The five winning plays will prepare you, motivate you, and energize you to positively impact your students. But that's not all. Your newfound knowledge, skills, and confidence will benefit you in life outside the classroom too.

So, why not plunge in? Simply turn the page to spark world-changing potential.

Be a Great Teacher by Friday

5 Winning Plays to Spark World-Changing Potential

Dr. Kevin Leman and Kristin Leman O'Reilly

BroadStreet
PUBLISHING

BroadStreet Publishing ® Group, LLC
Savage, Minnesota, USA
BroadStreetPublishing.com

Be a Great Teacher by Friday: 5 Winning Plays to Spark World-Changing Potential
Copyright © 2025 KAL Enterprises, Inc. & Kristin Leman O'Reilly

9781424568345 (hardcover)
9781424568352 (ebook)

Scripture quotations taken from the Holy Bible, New International Version® NIV®. Copyright © 1973, 1978, 1984, 2011 by Biblica, Inc. Used with permission. All rights reserved worldwide.

Editors: Ramona Cramer Tucker, Michelle Winger

To protect the privacy of those who have shared their stories with the authors, details and names have been changed.

Stock or custom editions of BroadStreet Publishing titles may be purchased in bulk for educational, business, ministry, fundraising, or sales promotional use. For information, please email orders@broadstreetpublishing.com.

Cover and interior by Garborg Design Works| garborgdesign.com

Printed in China

25 26 27 28 29 5 4 3 2 1

To my precious teacher,
Ms. Eleanor Wilson,
whose insight and challenging wisdom
enabled me to turn my life
in a positive direction.
Dr. Kevin Leman

To Dennis, Conner, and Adeline,
who have taught me how to love deeply
and to be the best version of myself.
Thank you for always believing in me.
You fill my heart with joy!
Kristin Leman O'Reilly

Contents

It's All About the 3 Rs

*You have an unparalleled opportunity
to positively impact the world.*

Want to help transform a life? You can! And as a teacher, you have the extraordinary opening to do that every day.

Whether you are considering teaching as a career, taking classes to become a teacher, neck-deep in being the new teacher on the block, or a veteran with lots of stories to tell, there is something you need to know. Teaching isn't just a *job*. If that's what it is to you, you won't stay in the field for long. Teaching is a lot of hard work, even with the perk of summers and major holidays off.

Instead, teaching is a *joy*. It's an unprecedented opportunity to be a difference-maker. It's your time to shine as you play a significant role in educating and training *up* the whole child into a responsible, caring member of society.

I am living proof of the results. You see, I was a clueless punk headed nowhere fast before I encountered the relational wisdom of a single teacher. She actually believed that the kid who drove teachers and administrators crazy could do something positive to help people, despite all evidence to the contrary.

For proof of that change, flash back with me to a few scenes of my growing-up years.

I Hated School

I hated everything about learning because it took place at school. I hated being stuck in a hard chair, staring at a board on the wall with squiggles that made no sense. I hated listening to teachers drone on and on about subjects I had no interest in. I ditched class anytime I could and high-tailed it to the creek for an appointment with my fishing pole.

On days I had to attend, school was as dull as mud. To overcome my boredom, I became the class clown who thrived on the peer reinforcement received for livening things up. What did I do? For starters, I made wild bird calls in class when the teacher wasn't looking. I crawled out of Mr. Giffen's world history class on my hands and knees. What's worse, poor Mr. Giffen didn't have a clue why the whole class was laughing.

I was also the central engineer of alarm clock day. Back then, alarm clocks were metal and dinged incessantly once set off. I rallied the majority of the school's population to bring an alarm clock, set it to 2:00 p.m., and place it in their locker. Imagine the racket and confusion that afternoon on behalf of teachers, staff, and administration.

Then there was newspaper day. Students brought newspapers and crumpled them in the main corridor of the high school. If I could generate some buzz and laughter before being sent to the principal's office, well, then it was a good day worth livin'.

Understandably, I did poorly in school. So poorly that I have a vivid memory of being in a first-grade reading group with a kid who ate paste. Yet as a six-year-old I thought, *I know I don't belong in this group.* I simply was not motivated. School was drudgery and the opposite of fun. Why should I engage?

I graduated high school near the bottom of my class, with my SAT scores near the 0 percentile. That didn't stop me from trying to apply to over 140 colleges and universities. While classmates got acceptances, no school wanted me. The church denomination I grew up in turned me down for their school too. As my high school counselor told me, "Leman, I couldn't get you admitted to reform school."

> School was drudgery and the opposite of fun.
> Why should I engage?

Then a miracle happened. Twelve days before the school semester was to start, I was admitted on probation with a 12-unit maximum load to North Park University in Chicago. My freshman year, I managed to eke out a C- average. To this day, I don't know how, since I'd never learned how to study.

However, during my sophomore year, my fun-loving nature kicked in a little too much. I stole the men's dorm "conscience fund" as a joke. The dean didn't find the prank funny and unceremoniously sent me packing.

Kicked out of the only school that would let me in, I moved to Tucson, Arizona, lived with my parents, and got a job as a janitor in a local hospital. On my lowest days I could admit that I was on a trajectory of heading nowhere fast.

What I Needed Most

A year and a half later, my life took a big turn at that same hospital. I met my future wife in, of all places, the men's restroom. Sande was a nurse's aide helping a patient. To say it was love at first sight is an understatement. I was dumbstruck in awe.

We married three-and-a-half years later with barely two shekels to rub together. Decades later, I still am amazed that a lady as classy as Sande would say yes to a guy like me who seemed to have nothing going for him. Besides giving me her heart and her hand, she gave me something else I desperately needed—someone to believe in me.

You see, while growing up, I didn't receive a lick of encouragement from any of my teachers, except for one glowing exception. In April of my senior year, Ms. Eleanor Wilson, an older teacher who had long observed my antics, pulled me aside for a private conversation.

I was certain I was in trouble…again. But Ms. Wilson had something else in mind.

"Kevin," she said kindly, "have you ever considered using your skills for something positive in life?"

I stared at her blankly. *Skills? I have skills?* No one had ever told me I had skills.

Ms. Wilson went on to tell me that she noticed how I thrived in the limelight and that others looked to me to make life fun. I had the ability to rally people together for a common cause, like getting the crowd to cheer as I ran out onto the field as the school mascot, and for making life memorable.

It was indeed an eye-opening conversation I will never forget.

To Ponder…

Individuals considered "impossible"
are waiting for you to show them
what's possible…and to believe in them
unconditionally during that transition.

Up until then, only one other person had stubbornly believed in me, despite me giving her every reason to doubt her sanity. Yes, you guessed it. It was my mother.

Mama Leman was a saint. She probably spent more time in the principal's office on my behalf than I did in class. Much later she confessed to me, "When you were in school, I prayed fervently for even one C to appear on your report card as a sign of life." I was a completely different act from my straight-A older sister and my star-athlete older brother.

Sande was the third person to believe in me. It was her love and belief, along with other life-changing experiences, that encouraged me to apply to the University of Arizona. Not only did I take a full load of classes, but I worked full-time and also made the Dean's List. I still remember staring at that list and then audibly saying my name, followed by, "It's a miracle."

Getting all As and Bs was incongruous for my educational history. But the spotlight of my motivation had been switched on, and I never looked back after that moment. I was in school for nearly 13 years straight, avidly soaking in knowledge, while simultaneously working to provide for my growing family.

As I discovered firsthand, sometimes people have a hard time seeing themselves as successful. It takes a little time for them to dream of what they could be, what they could do. To have the courage to ask, *Where would I like to be 10 years from now? How can I get there? What is attainable?* I was a perfect test subject for that.

LEMANISM #1

Lasting self-worth comes when kids know
they belong to a community and realize,
I can contribute. I can give something back.

All It Takes Is One Person to Believe in You

If my former teachers had seen me after my motivation switched on, they probably would have scratched their heads and questioned their ability to recall events correctly. I can imagine the buzz. *Kevin Leman…you mean THE Kevin Leman who used to cause all that trouble in school and literally drove a teacher out of teaching…he's doing WHAT?*

I powered on to earn my bachelor's, master's, and doctorate degrees at the University of Arizona. While there, I served as Assistant Director of High School Relations—imagine that—where I assisted in establishing the University's New Start program for students with economic challenges. The program, still going strong, has assisted over 4,000 individuals in receiving their bachelor's degrees.

Ten years after I'd been thrown out of one school, I served as Assistant Dean of Students at another. Little student manipulation got past me, since I knew all the tricks anyone might try. My firsthand knowledge in what to do and what not to do in motivating students came in handy. I also taught graduate-level counseling-in-practice classes for the College of Education. Later, the University of Arizona presented me with the Alumni Achievement Award, the highest award they can give one of their own.

For a final stroke of irony, North Park University, the same school that gave me my walking papers for stealing the "conscience fund," invited me back to award me a Doctorate of Humane Letters. All these happenings prove not only God Almighty's sense of humor but also the power of having individuals believe in you, despite a volume of evidence to the contrary.

> Ten years after I'd been thrown out of one school, I served as Assistant Dean of Students at another.

The Launch of a Dream

The impact of that single teacher's belief that I had skills—and her ability to pull me aside for a surprising, relational conversation at a deeply vulnerable time in my life—stirred the embers of transformation. Those embers, backed by my mother's continual encouragement and the love-of-my-life's belief in me, fanned into a flame of motivation. Years later, my hatred of school also sparked an educational dream to launch a school for kids like me who might otherwise be lost in the weeds.

The kind of school

- that is based on the key principles of respect, accountability, individuality, communication, and partnership between student, teacher, and the home.

- that creatively and happily motivates school-haters, transforming them into voracious life-long learners.

- where encouragement reigns, and learning is fun.

- where education is done in a safe environment, devoid of bullying and put-downs, and students are treated and treat others in the way in which they would like to be treated.

- where teachers are excellent in their craft, really care about their students, and emphasize the uniqueness and giftedness of every individual in their classes.

- where expectations of students are very high but also manageable and encourage personal-best achievement.

- that proactively prepares students for life beyond the classroom with practical skills for everyday living, such as good manners, self-discipline, respect for others, and basic etiquette.

- where students, parents, teachers, and administration all communicate respectfully and work together for the best possible education in all areas.

However, such a school cannot exist without committed, passionate teachers who love education and have students' long-term best in mind. Such teachers are the key to every single one of my dream points. Teachers must share the school's mission to train *up* children, model the established core values and beliefs, and live out the beneficial character traits that make education a partnership in a safe, stimulating learning environment.

An Apple a Day

Recall a teacher who made a difference in your life. Why not sweeten her day via email, snail-mail, or social media with the unexpected gift of encouragement?

Any teacher will be overjoyed that you remember her and took the time to contact her. Knowing how her investment in you has paid dividends will make her smile for a long time.

Bring On the Transformation

Transformations begin when competent, enthusiastic teachers, staff, and administrators form a learning environment that willingly engages and embraces students and those in their homes in the educational process. Take, for instance, the typical after-school conversation that occurs between many parents and children.

Parent: What did you learn at school today?

Child: Nothin'. *Child shrugs and begins texting on their cell phone.*

Now imagine this lively interaction that takes place instead with no prodding:

Child: *Bounces into the SUV, runs off the bus, or flings open the front door at home with excitement.* Guess what I learned at school today?!

Parent: Oooh, sounds like you learned something new and exciting. Tell me more. I'm all ears. I've got a snack prepared so we can eat and talk.

Yes, that miraculous transition can happen even with parents who have children in the teen zone. We know because we see it happen every day. Highlighting the student-parent-teacher relationship brings out the best in the student, which then pays dividends in the parent-child relationship and communication in the home.

That means you not only have the ability to positively influence a single student's trajectory but the trajectory of an entire family. That family then can choose to beneficially change others' trajectories. That's why we say that teachers—equipped with the five winning plays in this book—have the unprecedented opportunity to change the world, starting with one student at a time. As a bonus, all it takes to launch that process is five days. You'll be a great teacher by Friday...guaranteed!

> You not only have the ability to positively influence a single student's trajectory but the trajectory of an entire family.

If that idea gets you excited, you've come to the right place. We wholeheartedly believe in education as a necessary tool to equip children for the future. But we also believe that without the 3 Rs, long-term success in education and the resulting transformation it sparks in individuals is highly unlikely.

What are the 3 Rs?

- Relationships

- Relationships

- Relationships

Yes, you read that right. Relationships are so important to your job as teacher that we've repeated the concept three times. Good relationships with your students, positive and productive relationships with those in their homes, and mutually beneficial relationships with your colleagues at school are critical to your success in the teaching field. That's why you'll find the important thread of developing relationships running all throughout this book.

Whether you are pursuing public, private, or home schooling, and no matter your age, stage, or position, *Be a Great Teacher by Friday* will provide you with practical information, time-tested advice, and the motivation you need to thrive as a teaching professional. It's your roadmap to the most important things you need to know about

- Establishing a solid foundation of education basics.

- Managing your classroom and constructing its culture to put you in the driver's seat of authority and also promote your students' active engagement with learning.

- Understanding each of your students and how to uniquely motivate them.

- The hows and whys of discipline vs. punishment, and why letting real-life consequences deal the life lesson works every time.

- The best ways to get and keep parents, grandparents, and any others in your students' homes in your court.

Along the way, we'll pack in some space for reflection ("To Ponder…"), nugget-sized memorable truths ("Lemanisms"), creative ideas that stimulate learning, promote relationships, solve problems, and up the fun quotient in your classroom ("An Apple a Day"), and much more.

Our "Top 15 Countdown for Teachers" on page 169 provides an easy wrap-up of key concepts you'll learn in this book. You might want to make a photocopy of them to post where you can see them every day.

Ready for a wild, informative ride? Then let's go!

Monday

Winning Play #1
Establish a Rock-Solid Foundation

*Knowing and assimilating these education basics
are critical first steps.*

Who was instrumental in your decision to become a teacher?

For me, it was Professor Nancy Berggren of North Park University in Chicago. She was an expert in her educational field who wanted to ensure her students were well equipped. She wanted them to know, understand, and remember the content of her classes well after the tests had been administered and the grades determined. After blue-book exams, she talked with each of us personally about areas that needed further clarification based on our answers.

Her classes were rigorous and packed with lively stories about her own teaching experiences that gave us peeks inside real life in the classroom. She crafted a fun, creative, collaborative learning environment. It modeled what a teacher of excellence does and ignited my passion for teaching.

She was also my student-teacher supervisor. At North Park, elementary education majors were required to have three different experiences in different types of schools in the Chicago area. Professor Berggren observed my teaching and determined my placements. Because she cared about placing each of us students with the right teacher at the right school, I was placed at a wonderful elementary school with a fabulous teacher who was the right fit for me. I student taught in kindergarten and loved every minute.

Professor Berggren was also relational. She cared about her students as individuals and stretched us to do our best. She delivered honest feedback rooted in encouragement, complete with a warm smile. She demonstrated genuine concern for our long-term success both personally and professionally. To this day, I think of how her contagious positivity has shaped me as a person and as an educator.

What about you? Why did you decide to pursue teaching as a career? Was it because of someone's encouragement or because you saw the value of education in others' lives? What factors played into your decision? No teacher or teacher-to-be will answer those questions exactly the same way. That's because the motivation to pursue the teaching field is usually deeply personal.

Willow, from a rural town in Tennessee, wanted to return home as a teacher. She believed that knowledge and opportunities could assist in providing wings for the children there, as well as improve the dire economic situation of the community.

Growing up in a multi-lingual home expanded Levi's desire for students to not only understand basic academic subjects but also develop as world citizens, understanding peoples, cultures, specific-to-region issues, and learning multiple languages.

> The motivation to pursue the teaching field is usually deeply personal.

For Elena, teaching as a career was never a question. Always an avid learner, Elena would excitedly share anything she'd discovered. As a young girl, she frequently instructed her stuffed animals and, when they could be caught and taught, her siblings.

Waylon's older brother and sister are first-hand examples of the benefits of education. His brother was the first in their extended family to attend college. Years of education paved the way to the kind of job that gave him a hefty paycheck, allowing him to assist his siblings on their own educational journeys. His sister used her business degree to launch a local non-profit that assists low-income elderly residents who live alone. Waylon was her right-hand helper until his move into teaching in another state.

Each of these individuals has vastly differing backgrounds and educational journeys. But they share in common their passion for education and awareness of how it can inform, expand, and transform lives. In this chapter we'll briefly explore some education basics: what education is at its heart, the unique traits of schools and how they impact you, and what students need most to learn effectively and grow wings to fly.

What Education Really Is

There's no lack of data on the purpose and myriad benefits of education. You wouldn't be pursuing the path you are on or reading this book unless you believed in the value of education. Education widens a child's world. Knowledge prompts the potential for understanding, expands the possibilities of career options, and leads to a host of opportunities for positive influence.

Students who work hard to achieve educational goals develop skills, build self-confidence, and learn critical thinking. Their growing problem-solving abilities help them turn weaknesses into strengths, which influences the way they tackle challenges later in life. Education assists students in becoming informed citizens who can see patterns in history and discern how present-day actions impact not only them but their families, communities, and nation. It allows interaction with cultures and customs, promoting understanding and respect for diversity.

What is at the heart of all these benefits? Stated simply, education is *learning how to learn.* We love Dorothy L. Sayers' take: "The sole end of education is simply this, to teach men and women how to learn for themselves…whatever instruction fails to do this is effort spent in vain."[1]

Schools exist to teach students how to learn so they can continue learning all their lives and put into practice what they've learned. If a school doesn't have that at its heart, then it isn't a school where you should invest your precious time. If a school does, then lucky you. You've found a place where you can hang your hat and stay awhile…or for your entire career.

> Stated simply, education is *learning how to learn.*

The Unique Traits of "Learning How to Learn" Schools

Schools should be able to clearly state who they are, how they are operated, and whether they are public, private, charter, home school, or other. They should explain briefly the purpose of their particular type of school and where the school or schools are located. They should state the admission policy, which dictates the range of their student pool, plus any other required fees if it is not a tuition-free school. If you are job-searching, eagle-eye the admission policy statement so you apply for schools that match your personal beliefs, values, and goals. Schools should also explain foundational principles for their educational philosophy, how they came about, and how that impacts the teachers, students, and the families in their care. All these statements are clues about the type of organization you are working for or might want to investigate working for.

Mission Statement

Schools should also have a concise mission statement. It should specify the model of education used, the reason that model was chosen, and the process of learning. It should stipulate the type of learning environment. It should identify the end goals for students and how the school will proceed in pursuing those goals.

A school's mission statement (sometimes called a "purpose statement" or "vision statement") will reveal the direction a specific school wants to go. You will need to know that statement and understand how to teach in accordance with the mission of the school you'll be working with. You will play a critical role in the school's trajectory overall. If you personally agree with and believe in the mission, you're much more likely to actively play a role in the school pursuing and achieving its vision.

An Apple a Day

Post your school's mission statement where you can see it every day. If your school doesn't have one, why not write one of your own?

There's nothing like seeing a mission statement every day to help you prioritize the myriad tasks and surprises that come with the honored role of teacher.

Core Values

Schools should also clarify what their core values are in regard to academics, relationships with students' home networks, and the treatment of children. Core values, which some schools may call "founding principles" or "beliefs," are statements that all teachers, staff, and administrators should agree to in order to have a safe, invigorating, and successful learning environment. They should state the school's view of education, students, goals, uniqueness and diversity, standards and expectations, and how discipline will be handled. Most of all, they should zero in on parameters for the student-to-student relationship, the student-to-teacher relationship, and the parent-student-teacher relationship.

What bar does the school set in regard to academic progress? How do they view success in academics? Is the high bar described as attainable by any student, or is there a focus on the achievement of a select percentage in the class? Are teachers mentioned as having a critical role in that process?

How does the school view parents of the student and their involvement at school? Does the school focus mainly on their authority over the student and briefly mention parental support? Or does the school highlight parents as an important factor in education and encourage active partnership and a flow of communication between school and home?

How does the school view children? As mere vessels to be filled with knowledge? Or as unique individuals with growing skills who are to be treated with respect? What does the school say they hope for in the education of children?

The wording of core values will emphasize what matters most to the school's founders and administration. It also gives clues to how students, teachers, and parents will be treated in any intense situation. And it allows a peek into situations in which you, as the teacher, may find yourself and how the school will assist you in solving any issues.

> ### *To Ponder...*
>
> Consider the core value statements
> of these two schools.
> What do they say to you about the
> expectations and treatment of students?
> *School 1:*
> This school is about excellence.
> We expect 10% of students to hit the high bar.
> *School 2:*
> This school is about excellence.
> We expect every student can and will
> maximize their learning potential.

Character Traits

Imagine for a minute what a perfect school day would look like....

Likely it would be a day where all students treat classmates with kindness. A day where they listen attentively as you explain a new topic and eagerly participate in discussion times. A day where they do assignments enthusiastically without prompting.

Well, you can't get there without training.

Today's schools should not stop at training the mind. They should also train the heart. They should intentionally highlight how they will train *up* their students. Which desired virtues or character attributes will they choose to focus on and hold students accountable for?

> ### *To Ponder...*
>
> The formation of habits is education,
> and education is the formation of habits.
> CHARLOTTE MASON

If a school overly focuses on disciplinary methods and makes little or no mention of encouraging beneficial character traits, you might want to ask specific questions about that discrepancy at your interview. The administrator's response will tell you a great deal about his or her attitude toward people who ask questions...and, ultimately, whether this job is one for you.

If you're already working at a school, and they don't yet have such a list, it could be because no one has ever put beneficial traits on paper. Why not step up to the plate and show your leadership skills? You could brainstorm with other teachers and then write a list of traits the school could employ to train up children.

When you submit it to administration for consideration, don't forget to credit all the teachers who helped brainstorm.

> Today's schools should not stop at training the mind. They should also train the heart.

Kindly explain your reasons upfront for drafting the list, including starting a discussion on this very important topic of education. Through this small act, you could spark the change you want to see in your school and make your own job easier in the long run.

Be Equipped, Be in the Know

If you're currently working for a school, do you know the school's mission statement, core values, and character attributes they strive for? Are such statements referred to regularly in teacher meetings and decisions the school makes? Are they displayed prominently so teachers, staff, administration, students, and parents have the opportunity to see them every day?

If you're looking for a teaching job, one of the most important things to look for as you evaluate school opportunities is an up-front, transparent mission statement, a listing of core values, and character traits. Such statements might be called by other titles, but the ideas should be spelled out and accessible. If a school doesn't have those, it's a rudderless boat that will flounder in the first big wave, and you'd be better off finding work elsewhere.

You deserve a school where you can flourish. A school that adheres to your personal values and supports your meaningful work. Your students deserve teachers who passionately agree with and regularly carry out the highest calling of the school. They also need daily doses of these essential vitamins that smart teachers dole out in healthy portions.

> You deserve a school where you can flourish. A school that adheres to your personal values and supports your meaningful work.

7 Essential Vitamins Your Students Need Every Day

For your students to grow to their full potential, they must have these vitamins that only you, as the authority in the classroom, can provide. Distribute these vitamins widely and wisely, along with the beneficial traits that the school you work for has intentionally chosen to highlight. Do so, and you'll be amazed at the transformation in students who might be considered "incorrigible"…one of the terms teachers used for the young Kevin Leman.

#1: Vitamin A = Accountability + Attitude

The best way to become responsible is to be given responsibility and then to be held accountable for completing that responsibility with a healthy attitude. Do you hold your students responsible for their actions? Do they have a good attitude about their tasks? Do you hold them accountable to manage those tasks, including adhering to provided deadlines? Is their contribution to the classroom a positive one?

Doing too much for your students and not holding them responsible and accountable for their attitude and actions will backfire. It will cause chaos in your classroom and hamper their long-term success as human beings of worth to the planet. Who wants a colleague down the road who has a bad attitude about his work? Who can't play well with others? Or who passes the buck of blame if caught not finishing projects on time?

LEMANISM #2

Don't fall for excuses.
Excuses make the weak weaker.

A hovered-over late-blooming plant will never bloom with too much watering. It will merely become limp and unable to stand up under harsh conditions in the real world. Do your students a favor. Give them responsibility. Hold them accountable. Set the roadmap in your classroom with clear guidelines and high expectations.

Then back off and let students make their own decisions. Will they be responsible? Will they be accountable? You can't *make* someone have a good attitude. Neither can you *make* them be responsible. But you can hold them accountable for their attitude and actions. The choice will be up to each individual whether they learn the hard way or the easy way.

The sooner your students learn that their attitude matters and that their choices have beneficial or detrimental consequences, the better. The sooner they learn that failing to be accountable garners negative consequences, but that finishing that project on time and doing your best leads to a sense of accomplishment and confidence, the better. The best place for students to learn the effects of responsibility, accountability, and attitude is in the safety of your classroom. The world after school won't be as forgiving.

To Ponder...

You cannot tailor-make the situations in life, but you can tailor-make the attitudes to fit those situations.

ZIG ZIGLAR

#2: Vitamin B = Behavioral Expectation

If you expect the worst, you'll likely get that. But if you expect the best, you're much more likely to get that. Why not expect the best to have the highest probability to get the best?

A student struggles to finish assignments. You pull him aside on a Wednesday. "I can't wait to see your science project," you say. "I've seen you work so hard for almost a month on it, and you've asked some very good questions too. You seem to like science. All that's left is the final stage now. If you want to run anything by me, I'm all ears. We could do a test run after school together tomorrow or Friday. Otherwise, I look forward to your presentation on Monday. The class can learn a lot from it." After such a conversation, chances are pretty high that student will show up prepared for that presentation.

Contrast that with this approach. A student constantly swivels and tries to engage another student in conversation, effectively distracting the entire class. You say, "John, turn around and face the front. Pay attention." Then you add the follow-up threat, "If you can't pay attention, I'll be forced to move your desk to the front of the classroom, and you'll sit there the rest of the day."

What have you done? You've actually planted the seed in that student's mind to continue to act up. In fact, you've added fuel to the fire. He can be more distracting to the entire class if he sits at the front. You will be the one swiveling to see what expressions and actions he's using as you attempt to teach the rest of the day.

Why not try a private, relational conversation that expects the best of a student instead of the worst? "John, I noticed that you seem to have difficulty sitting in your chair with your feet pointing toward the front. Maybe you have a reason for this that I should know about. If so, I'd like to understand it. Perhaps I could help in solving the issue."

If you prime your students to act up by expecting the worst out of them, you shoot yourself in the foot. If you name a follow-up threat if they don't comply, you shoot yourself in the foot again. You'll be forced to comply with the threat, or you'll lose control of your classroom. Why do that to yourself?

Instead, try great expectations. They don't guarantee you'll *always* get the best, but they can make a great difference. Try them out and see.

LEMANISM #3

Students live up to the expectations
you have for them.

#3: Vitamin C = Caring + Cooperation

A tough-as-nails but good-hearted football coach once told me about his players, "They don't care what you know...until they know that you care." The same goes for your students. They don't care what you know, or what you think, or what you say until they know you care.

Your relationship with your students is critical to their ability to learn. It influences the role they perceive they have in your classroom. That perception influences how they engage with your teaching, respond to assignments, interact with their peers, and perform on tests.

The words you choose to say directly impact how willing your students are to listen. They also impact how willing they are to be healthy contributors to the group as a whole. Caring means getting behind each of your student's eyes to the way he or she views the world and then having heart-to-heart, one-on-one conversations that uniquely connect with each student. These

> The words you choose to say directly impact how willing your students are to listen.

30

connections are so important, in fact, that we'll spend a later chapter on them.

Caring means being available for and welcoming individual conversation. It means being sensitive to what matters to each student. It means being the calm in their storms. Yes, it's a tall order with a full class. But there is no replacement for a caring teacher.

LEMANISM #4

You must win
your students' cooperation.

#4: Vitamin D = Discipline

Each of us makes mistakes. Each of us has flaws. Each of us needs some fine-tuning in our attitudes and behaviors from time to time. But there's a big difference between punishing a student and disciplining a student.

Punishment handles mistakes and flaws in a way that trains *down* a student. It focuses on the need to make a student pay for a specific behavior that has negative consequences. However, punishment is a temporary fix. It attempts to take care of the current situation but does not address the reason for the underlying behavior. Without that reason being addressed, such behavior is bound to happen again, no matter the consequences.

Punishment also has a high "oops" factor. Typically punishment is served cold, with a twist of emotion. After all, there's a reason a particular student is driving you a little nuts. Time and again, he has been the primary instigator of this type of behavior in your classroom. In this situation he is implicated again. You didn't catch him in the act, but understandably you're annoyed. With punishment, you don't give yourself the opportunity to ask, *What if he isn't the culprit this time? What if there is a better way to handle this?*

Discipline handles mistakes and flaws in a positive manner that trains *up* a student. Disciplining a student prompts him to halt negative behavior as a result of natural consequences for that particular behavior. It allows him the freedom to accept the consequences and work to address any harm that might have resulted from his actions or attitude. It gives the student the opportunity to *choose* to make amends and then *choose* to respond differently the next time. Discipline grows both mind and heart. As such, it has the potential for long-term character growth that will benefit the student beyond the present classroom.

An Apple a Day

What would you do in the following situations?

1. Your student exhibits an attitude that influences other students to jump on the ol' bandwagon.
   Option A (Punishment): Send him to detention. In fact, send them *all* to detention.
   Option B (Discipline): (You do the brainstorming).

2. It's clear your student spent about five minutes on homework that should have taken 20-30 minutes. You know she can do better.
   Option A (Punishment): Take away her brain break of recess and make her redo it.
   Option B (Discipline): (You do the brainstorming).

3. Your student failed to turn in his test paper before walking out the door.

   Option A (Punishment): Give him a big fat 0 in your grade book.

   Option B (Discipline): (You do the brainstorming).

Discipline has a student's best in mind. It not only allows but encourages the formation of good habits. But a student's acceptance of discipline starts with you.

Do you model a disciplined life? Do you finish tasks you dread or procrastinate on them? Do you do what you say you will do, when you say you will do it? Do you stay balanced and steady instead of allowing life's occurrences to throw you? Do you readily say you're sorry when you're in the wrong? Do you try to make amends to the best of your ability?

The instant you step into a teaching position, you become a role model. Your students are watching you. What you do will shout more loudly than what you say. Your relationship with them makes all the difference. That's why we believe so highly not only in discipline but in *relational discipline,* a subject we'll explore in a later chapter.

To Ponder...

The question is not,
Am I teaching my students habits?
The question is,
Which habits am I teaching my students?

#5: Vitamin E = Encouragement

There's a mountain of difference between *praise* and *encouragement.* Even dictionaries know. Take a look.

Praise
1. To express a favorable **judgment** of.
2. To glorify especially by the attribution of **perfections.**
3. An expression of **approval.**[2]

Encouragement
1. The action of giving someone **support, confidence,** or **hope.**
2. The act of trying to **stimulate** the development of an activity, state, or belief.[3]
3. To **inspire with courage.**[4]

Note the words highlighted in bold for *praise: judgment, perfections,* and *approval.* Praise sounds like it would be positive, but it's actually a negative tool. It focuses on the student and how he or she measures up. It involves expectations and sets the student up for a fall.

Now note the words highlighted in bold for *encouragement: support, confidence, hope, stimulate, inspire with courage.* Encouragement is positive, through and through. It focuses on the deed or action and on how the student feels about that action.

Here's an example of the differences in a real-life situation:

Praise: "You won the spelling bee. You are the best speller in the entire school!"

Encouragement: "All that studying you did sure paid off. I bet you feel a huge sense of accomplishment. Congrats on winning the spelling bee."

Kids can't be fooled. They instinctively know there's a chasm between praise and encouragement. When you tell a student, "You're the best (whatever)," he knows that's not true. Yes, he might have received the top grade on the history test that day. However, the next day someone may come along and knock him right off his pedestal.

Praise puts any student in a precarious position. She will feel the stress of maintaining that position every day. She may become very driven to succeed, like the straight-A student caught using AI to write her final paper in high school. Or she may sink into procrastination out of fear of being criticized for failing to reach the high bar every time, like the talented athlete or musician who is either always late or doesn't come to practice at all.

> Praise = NO
> Encouragement = YES

A child who feels the internal success of knowing she did something well as a result of her hard work will always outshine in the long-term the child who is praised for who she is. That's because the sweetest words to a child's heart connote: "I care about you. I believe in you. I have confidence in you. I know you can do this."

So, lavish on the encouragement. You can never overdo it. Use statements like, "Wow, that took a lot of research, but you figured it out. All that hard work really paid off." And, "I love seeing you digging into a project and finishing it with such flair. That has to feel great inside."

To Ponder...

Let my teaching fall like rain
and my words descend like dew,
like showers on new grass,
like abundant rain on tender plants.

DEUTERONOMY 32:2

#6: Vitamin L = Laughter

Laughter is an essential ingredient to a well-rounded classroom. Having fun together gels students as a group, provides acceptance and belonging, and lessens the probability of inter-student disputes. The class that plays together is more likely to have each other's backs on the playground. Members feel more comfortable in sharing ideas and discoveries and form friendships.

So, why not laugh it up every chance you can get? You'll all enjoy the moment before you get back to the subject at hand. Your students will have something hilarious to share at home. Word will get around , and other students will wish they were in "the fun class." Who knows? Other teachers might be emboldened and risk lightening up a little too.

#7: Vitamin N = No

No is not a dirty word. It is, in fact, not only useful but necessary in the classroom. Not everything is beneficial, nor is it healthy. Should danger be imminent, safety must come first. Drawing clear guidelines and boundaries is critical to providing a safe classroom.

With boundaries students know what to expect. It's a simple A + B = C equation. If they do this and this, then this is the result. There's no nagging, yelling, cajoling, or reminding. The response has been pre-set.

Will your students always be happy with Vitamin N? No. But a healthy child is not always a happy child.

LEMANISM #5

A healthy child is not always a happy child.

Always saying yes because you have a need to be a beloved teacher doesn't produce a happy class. It fosters an unsettled, boundaryless environment populated with unhappy children who think the world always owes them a yes. Painting school and life in general as an easy romp does students a disservice. It's an illusion that won't hold up.

When should you say yes, and when should you say no? Say yes when you can and the situation allows for it. Save your no for what really matters and make it clear. You lessen the potential for argument when students know your no means no and that you won't back down. Such behavior also increases the safety quotient, leaving your students free to explore their potential talents without wondering what will happen next. They can try and succeed, or try and fail. Either route occurs in a supportive environment where putdowns and bullying are not tolerated.

Redefining Success

What is your definition of a successful teacher? One whose students all get top scores on the year-end tests or out-perform other classes in the same grade by a mile? Whose students go on to become top-performing students in subsequent grades and later become CEOs, top-rated engineers, or heads of schools?

If that's your definition of success, you'll always feel a little stressed and competitive with your colleagues. And kids aren't dumb. They'll feel that tension and discern your motives. It will translate to them as, *Oh, I see. All she really cares about is the grade I get, so it doesn't mess up her score. She doesn't really care about me.*

Whatever stress you feel, the perfectionist firstborns and only kids will double it for themselves. The middleborns will think, *Well, I can't measure up to that, so why try? I'll do my own thing and stay out of the way as much as I can. Flyin' under the radar is the best way to operate.* The babies of the family will figure, *She cares about grades, huh? Then let's mess up her good student average and see what happens next. It oughta be more entertaining than this boring class.*

It's easy to view success in a tinsel-like manner. But success will look different for each of your students. One student might have worked long hours to learn to read…a skill that might have come naturally to a classmate at school. Finally, he can read a whole short chapter by himself and earns an award. Another might have struggled with understanding the concepts of science and finally achieves a passing grade in the subject. The third student might have repeated a grade due to the lack of ability to grasp key concepts and high stress in the home. This time around he's getting it.

So, how about adopting these definitions of success instead:

- When students show steady improvement during the year, learn key skills and become proficient at them, and exit the year having done their personal bests.

- When students grapple with subjects that are difficult for them, work hard to achieve that B at the end of the year, and share their excitement and thanks with you because they value and respect you as their teacher.

- When your students go on to the next grade with a good work ethic, a healthy camaraderie with their classmates due to their side-by-side work, and a happy expectation of what they'll learn that year.

- When the student who struggled intensely with his times table in math returns to school years later to tell you that he's decided to pursue accounting in college and confides that he might even become a math teacher, like you.

- When your fourth graders surround you at the end of the year for a group hug and tell you they love you and will miss you.

If you've experienced any of those mile-markers, you're already a successful teacher.

For, you see, success isn't really about achievement that others can measure on the outside. It's about developing greatness on the inside. It's about assisting your students to become people who have the kind of character, passion, and work ethic that will help them confidently tackle challenges, power over obstacles, and treat others as they would want to be treated.

> Success isn't really about achievement that others can measure on the outside. It's about developing greatness on the inside.

Those kids working hard for their personal-best achievements? Such serendipities will make any teacher smile. The way your students feel about those awards, those passing grades, and promotions to the next level? About finding the career they might love to study? Those joyful feelings are also yours. You're the motivator, the leader of the pack. Go ahead, pat yourself on the back, because you deserve it.

Remember, success is a long-term game. As educators, let's play to win for our students' sake.

Tuesday

Winning Play #2
Manage Your Classroom
and Craft Its Learning Culture

*Balancing healthy authority and support
with high expectations promotes active engagement.*

Are you managing your class, or is your class managing you?

Does the pace of your lesson fall off the cliff because of chatty students? Do you find it hard to get the class under control after doing a fun activity? Do you wonder where all the class time goes when you're unable to get through the curriculum? Do students get quiet every time you ask them questions?

If you've struggled with any of those questions and more, you're not alone. Classroom management is likely the hardest aspect of teaching for any teacher. After all, you are placed in charge of an active roomful of students, and the composition of that class changes every year. It's a complex puzzle that can keep you on your toes. Shall we be frank between us teachers?

If you aren't managing those students, they are busy managing you. The stress of that can really wear you down. But it doesn't have to be that way. You can put yourself in the driver's seat with the effective tools we'll provide in this chapter. They'll help you do the heavy lifting all year long. Not only that, they're easily implemented.

> If you aren't managing those students, they are busy managing you.

This chapter will help you establish healthy authority over your classroom and show you what that looks like. It'll assist you in cultivating an energetic learning atmosphere. And it will help you effectively manage your room, time, and materials. Before you know it, you'll be happily in charge of your classroom, highly organized, carefully planned, and adequately prepared for each lesson. You'll reclaim your weeknights and weekends for yourself, family, and friends.

Doesn't that sound good? If so, read on.

To Ponder...

We are what we repeatedly do.
Excellence is not an act, but a habit.

ARISTOTLE

Three Types of Classroom Management Styles

When you step into a classroom, you are empowered to be the authority of that classroom. What you do with that empowerment, however, is up to you. Will you allow your students to work you, or will you choose to be in healthy authority over them?

Kids instinctively know which buttons to push to get you to perform like a trained seal in an aquatic show. Like the sixth-graders who knew their teacher loved to talk about his experiences in the army. If they could get him talking about his experiences, they knew he'd forget to assign them homework. Or the college juniors in behavioral psychology class who had learned different ways of reinforcing behaviors and tried it out one day on their good ol' professor. As he lectured, they picked an arbitrary place in the middle of the classroom. When he moved to that spot, all eyes focused on him. As soon as he stepped away from that spot, students would act distracted and would stop focusing on him. Within 10 minutes he was lecturing from way back in the corner, where their experiment had taken him.

Kids are smart…and far smarter than you give them credit for. Having a presence of authority in the classroom is important. It starts with the first day you walk into the place. Kids will read you like a good student would read their notes before a big exam. And they're awfully insightful.

Teachers can be grouped into three categories regarding how they use authority. As you read the following, ask yourself:

- *Which classroom management style sounds most like me right now?*

- *Which classroom management style sounds like one I'd like to work toward?*

The type of management style you're using now doesn't mean you have to continue using that style if you see more benefit in another style. After all, every action you take as a result of this book is your choice. Remember, this book is all about starting where you are on a Monday and working your way to becoming a great teacher by Friday. Only by recognizing and acknowledging where you are *right now* in your skills can you move in that direction.

> When you step into a classroom, you are empowered to be the authority of that classroom. What you do with that empowerment, however, is up to you.

Having a learning-for-a-lifetime attitude will take you far. We'll not only help you project where you want to be but give you the steps to take you there. So, let's get right to it, shall we?

The Authoritarian Teacher

Have you ever entered a room and immediately felt a chill? We're not talking about the air-conditioning or a fan creating a cool environment. We're talking about the feeling in the air.

Well, school classrooms are the same way. We can walk in the door of any school classroom and, within the first few seconds, have a pretty good sense of the type of authority the teacher has. How is that possible? No, we're not part bloodhound. Instead, we've learned that each type of authority creates a temperature in the classroom.

Imagine walking the halls of a school and hearing a teacher's voice booming from a middle-school classroom. Curious, you step in and investigate what is going on. The class is being chewed out. The teacher is up front, and his face is red. He is threatening the class that they need to stop talking or else. Students look scared. There's not a peep being made by anyone but the angry teacher.

Instinct takes over. You approach the teacher and ask how you can help.

He retorts, "They just don't listen."

This is a classic authoritarian classroom management style. The teacher does not own any responsibility for his poor lesson plans, lack of preparedness, or the low behavioral expectations that he has created for the class. He thinks his mere presence in the room is enough authority to run the classroom and that he can control the behavior of his students with a demonstrative attitude.

A "do what I say because I said so" management style literally screams authoritarianism. This style is based on controlling through fear and threats. Students either submit because they are afraid, or they rebel inwardly or outwardly. They have little or no relationship with the teacher. In fact, the teacher may not know all of their names.

Teachers who use an authoritarian style are quick to criticize. They meet a putdown with another putdown. They compare one student to another or that student's sibling from an earlier class. They leap to conclusions before they hear the whole story. They believe there is only one way to do things—the right way—and that's their way. They feel driven to get in the last word. They have to be the one who is in control at all times. Control defines them and makes them who they are.

Authoritarian teachers tend to make declarative statements to control their classroom, such as, "Get your desks cleaned in the next five minutes." They also tend to add additional statements such as, "I'm not going to say it twice."

> Authoritarian teachers tend to make declarative statements to control their classroom.

Issuing an order and combining it with a warning may, at first glance, seem to make logical sense. After all, students can be contrary. However, when you make such statements, what are you really saying to your students? "I'm telling you to do something on a short timeframe, but I don't really expect you to do it. I expect to have to tell you to do it more than once since I know you won't listen." Your tone can also dictate that you feel your opinion is the only one that matters.

Negative expectations don't curb off-task behavior or rebellion. They actively invite it. Here's what the most enterprising students will think: *Ah, that's the way you roll. Let's see if I can make you say it not only twice, but more.*

Students learn swiftly how to bait authoritarian teachers and enjoy devising ways of how such a teacher will fall into their trap. I ought to know. I did it all the time when I was growing up. It

> Negative expectations don't curb off-task behavior or rebellion. They actively invite it.

was great fun to engineer situations where I could watch a certain teacher's forehead vein throb and his face turn an apoplectic red.

Using an authoritarian style at first seems easy. You give what you believe is a clear order and resulting consequences in one fell swoop. If that task isn't done, you bring the hammer down. For example, "This morning I told you that we could go outside this afternoon for a 15-minute break if you stayed on task during math time. Well, you've lost that break."

At the core of the authoritarian method is fear or anger that your teaching methods or authority will be challenged. You are, after all, the teacher. You can't let any student or group of students rout that authority.

An authoritarian style of teaching might accomplish the purpose of forced education due to tight control in the classroom. However, it misses the boat on building relationships in the classroom. Without relationships, students won't receive the full benefit of learning to apply in practice what they've learned. And let's be honest, shall we? Low expectations and hammer wielding will exact its toll on you physically and emotionally too. It's not the way to fly if you want to stay in this career long-term.

The Permissive Teacher

Permissive teachers are as easy to spot as a red stain on a white carpet.

Imagine that you are called in to assist a teacher who is struggling with establishing her authority in the classroom. Upon entering the room, you note that it is very messy. The students are busily doing myriad off-task activities, such as cleaning their desks and walking around chatting with each other. Worse yet, the teacher is not teaching.

When the teacher does try to teach, she repeatedly asks the students to stop talking. The common refrain of a permissive teacher is, "Come on, guys, please. Let's just get through this."

She then proceeds to beg, plead, and bargain with her class to do what she wants them to do.

Afterward, you talk with the teacher. You suggest that you model teaching a lesson with that same group of students. The next day, you do that. She observes, and you teach. The students get quiet, focus, and actively engage in their learning.

> The common refrain of a permissive teacher is, "Come on, guys, please. Let's just get through this."

The teacher observes and takes a lot of notes. She's curious how you can manage the same group of students in a way that she can't...yet. She also observes another teacher's class and is so impressed with how smoothly everything goes. The students listen as that teacher talks and actively engage. She tells you, "Wow, that teacher has an easy class."

But she continues to have the same issues in her classroom. You invest weeks coaching her how to establish a healthy authority in her class. The traction you make feels minimal at best. Something has to change. You call a post-conference after school. It's time to get to the root of the matter.

In your private meeting you move your notes to the side and ask her to do the same thing. You look her in the eye and ask a critical question: "Why do you think you are struggling to hold your students accountable?"

She looks puzzled. Then, after a few minutes, she says quietly, "I think it's because I really want to be liked by my class." The story of her background pours out. She finishes the story by saying, "I vowed to never act like my dad treated me growing up."

Whoa! The heart of the issue is at last uncovered. She looks relieved, as if a weight has been lifted off her shoulder.

It's time for what we call the "teachable moment," that time ears are fully open and both heart and mind are ready for the truth. You say, "Did you know it is *healthy* to hold your students accountable?" You explain how it can be done in a healthy manner, unlike what she experienced at home with her father.

This time she is able to fully hear what you say. The psychological cobwebs have at last been cleared away. The next week she tries the techniques you describe. Things slowly begin to turn around in her class. Students begin to listen as she talks. They start to actively engage with their learning. She now smiles in the hallway and whispers to you, "It's a miracle…."

Teachers with a permissive style tend to bribe or cajole students into doing what they want. They allow their students to take advantage of them. They ask students to do something and often end up doing it themselves. They tend to have favorite students. Their self-worth is based on whether others, including students, parents, and colleagues, like them or not.

Permissive teachers don't like to challenge behaviors head-on like authoritarians do. Instead they offer bonuses to motivate their students to stay on task. They also have a great deal of empathy. They tend to cave, waffle, or back down when faced with consequences for off-task behavior. They give additional chances or tend to repeat themselves: "Okay, class, I said it's time to get your desks cleaned up."

Students are still talking 10 minutes later instead of completing that task. What does the teacher say? "If you get your desks cleaned, I'll add *another* five minutes to our break time." That's like holding out a carrot to a fluffle of bunnies that don't really like or need carrots. They aren't likely to pay attention.

Students learn fast how to wrap permissive teachers around their pinky fingers. The teacher tells the class in the morning that they can take a break in the afternoon if they stay on task during math time. More enterprising students think, *Okay, I know how to get a whole half hour more of break. All we have to do is milk this a little….*

Guess what? Those students become masterful manipulators, pulling that teacher's puppet strings. Sure enough, the permissive teacher caves mid-afternoon. "All right, let's go take that break now. After all, it's so nice outside. Remember to pay attention next time during math."

At the core of the permissive style is the need to be liked by your students. You struggle to discipline them because you are trying overly hard to be your students' friend. You go out of your way to rescue them from consequences. You over-remind them of deadlines. You change deadlines and try to sweeten the deal. You rarely follow through on threats or requests.

But let's be honest: It is not humanly possible to be liked by every person all the time. Your job is not to provide a Fantasyland experience for your students. Sometimes they will have to suffer consequences for their own actions. Such consequences are often inconvenient or uncomfortable in order to learn, *Wow, I certainly won't do that again.*

> Your job is not to provide a Fantasyland experience.

The Authoritative Teacher

Imagine that you are walking down a crowded school hallway. You notice that Kinsley, a middle-school student, is holding what appears to be a much-younger child's toy. You know Kinsley well, and she doesn't have any younger siblings. She also hangs with the "cool kid" crowd and doesn't seem the type to own such an item. You ponder all those things as you continue on with your day.

After school, you run into a kindergartener, Zoey, and her mom searching the Lost & Found. They're looking desperately for the toy you saw Kinsley holding that morning. The puzzle pieces fall into place.

You quietly tell the family that you know who has the toy and promise it will be returned tomorrow. Then you high-tail it to Kinsley's class. As she exits, you pull her aside privately and ask about the toy you saw her with at her locker.

She admits uncomfortably that she found it on the playground and decided to take it. Because of your previous relationship, when you were her teacher, and her trust in you, she goes on to tell you the back story. She always wanted a toy like that, but she was never able to have one. Her family couldn't afford it.

When you ask Kinsley to return it, she hangs her head. "I would, but I accidentally broke it, so I threw it away," she says. You know her, and you believe her. She's a good kid who had a moment of poor judgment. It happens. What's most important is what you do next.

You tell Kinsley there's someone you want her to meet and escort her to the kindergarten classroom. After swiftly explaining the situation to the kindergarten teacher and asking him if you can borrow Zoey for a moment, you gather the two students in the hallway for a quick chat. You intro-

> She's a good kid who had a moment of poor judgment. It happens. What's most important is what you do next.

duce the two students to each other and then tell Zoey, "Kinsley has something to say to you."

Embarrassed, Kinsley says she took a toy from the playground, accidentally broke it, and threw it away. When Zoey realizes the toy was hers, she looks devastated. You ask Kinsley what she would suggest to remedy this situation. She tells the kindergartener, "I'll get you a new one."

You escort both students back to their classrooms, then phone Kinsley's parent and explain the situation. He is calm and incredibly supportive. He tells you he is disappointed in his daughter's behavior, especially since it seems very unlike her, and sees now as the chance to hold her accountable for her actions before the stakes are higher. He says he will create a list of tasks Kinsley will have to do over the next few weeks to earn the money for the toy.

Kinsley works every day after school for three weeks. You notice that she seems tired when you see her in the hallway outside her home room. Then one morning she shows up at school with the new toy in hand. She searches you out and gives it to you. You put the toy right back into her hands and say, "Let's walk together to the kindergarten classroom."

After again asking the kindergarten teacher's permission, you and the two girls meet again in the hallway. Kinsley apologizes again for taking the toy, then shyly hands Zoey the new toy. Zoey breaks into a huge smile, hugs Kinsley, and thanks her. You'll never forget the teachable moment emblazoned on their faces: relief on Kinsley's, joy on Zoey's.

After Zoey returns to class, you walk with Kinsley across campus to her class. On the way, you thank her for owning her part in this situation. You tell her you are proud of her for persevering and doing the right thing. Right afterwards you phone her dad to say the toy has been delivered and thank him for his intentional role in resolving the situation and allowing a life lesson.

A week later you smile as you watch the two students talking and laughing together on the playground at lunchtime. By allowing natural consequences to play out, both students learned powerful lessons that included respect for each other and others' possessions, doing the right thing even when it's difficult, problem-solving face-to-face, hard work, and forgiveness. As a bonus, an unlikely friendship might be budding.

Teachers with an authoritative management style teach and model respect for everyone at school. They hold students accountable for their actions and let the ball of responsibility land in the right court. They let reality, rather than lectures, do the teaching regarding consequences. They treat students as contributors to their class and the school as a whole.

> Let the ball of responsibility land in the right court.

Authoritative teachers also earn respect by being fair, not dictatorial and not a pushover. They do what they say they'll do and when they say they'll do it. How students perform does not inform how authoritative teachers feel about themselves or their performance. They realize that detrimental consequences for actions are simply a fact of life. However, they choose to use such occurrences as teaching tools.

LEMANISM #6
Deciding not to act
is also an action.

Authoritative teachers know how to use their empowered authority to their own and their students' best learning advantage in the classroom. The authoritative teacher sets up precedents and rules in her classroom at the beginning of the school year to cover processes and expectations. Her yes is yes, and her no is no. She doesn't need to say either twice, because students know she will follow through in doing what she says. Her answer will not change. If a student does not hear the directions and asks the teacher to say them again, the authoritative teacher calmly says that she gave her directions. The student will have to "phone a friend" to hear them again.

Let's replay the desk cleaning and staying on task during math-time situations from an authoritative style.

Scenario #1. You set positive expectations early in the year that desk and room cleaning will happen regularly the last 20 minutes of every Friday. At that time, students automatically jump to those tasks without any reminder. If they get cleaning done well and swiftly, they know their routine efforts will be recognized and acknowledged with a smile from you. As members of the classroom community, all work together as a group to leave their classroom neat and clean on Friday so they can enter ready to learn on Monday. Besides, it feels really good to be able to start fresh every week.

Scenario #2. Your students are guided by your positive, high expectations. You expect that they will pay attention during class. Students learn that exhibiting such beneficial behaviors might lead to an occasional surprise. "Well, class, don't you think it's a lovely day? Close your books. We work hard so we can play hard." Then off you go after math-time for a 15-minute break in the afternoon sunshine.

> Your students are guided by your positive, high expectations. You expect that they will pay attention during class.

Note that you wisely clarify exactly *what* prompted the surprise break: their hard work. Such wording squarely places your students in the driver's seat of their own behavior. Whether that surprise happens or not is not based on your feelings. It's based on your students' motivation and the ability to stay on-task. If students stay on-task, you might have time for a break. If they don't stay on-task, time runs out for what they need to learn, so there's no opportunity for a break. Words of affirmation and the fun quotient go a long way for intrinsic motivation and in growing your relationship with your students.

Scenario #3. Early in the day, you tell your students you expect that you will be able to take a short break at 2:00 in the afternoon, as long as you can all stay on-task during math. Your students choose off-task behaviors instead of concentrating on their lessons. You don't cajole, bribe, plead, or remind them about the break. In fact, you say nothing further about it at all. You simply let reality play out, complete with choices and consequences.

At 2:00 p.m. you go on with the lesson at hand. You allow the break time to pass and ignore the rustlings of students in their chairs. You simply wait for the teachable moment, when eyes are open and ears are ready to hear the truth.

We assure you, that teachable moment won't take long to arrive. After a glance at classmates for support, one student will raise his hand. "Uh, Teacher, weren't we supposed to go outside?"

"Yes, that was the plan," you say calmly. "But we didn't meet our goal today during math. So, turn to page…."

There is no further explanation. No waffling and giving in. No opportunity for students to debate the decision. No chance for them to grumble about your decision being unfair. They all know they weren't on-task during math.

> You simply wait for the teachable moment, when eyes are open and ears are ready to hear the truth.

Life goes on. The break is missed. Students now know that you mean business. They also know that they are squarely in the drivers' seat of their own actions. What they choose to do has natural consequences. The sense of deflation after losing out on a sunshine-filled break is a powerful learning tool that will encourage beneficial behavior in the future.

LEMANISM #7
Stick to the plan and don't deviate from it.

There's another side benefit to sticking to the plan too. Peer pressure is typically viewed as bad. However, there's a beneficial side to caring what your peers think. If there is one student in the bunch who engages in off-task behavior that results in a loss for the group, it's likely he'll swiftly face some real-life peer counseling about that behavior not being acceptable. No student wants to be on the contrary side of his peers for long.

The 3 Classroom Management Styles

Authoritarian: "Do what I say or else."
Permissive: "Do what I say…if you want."
Authoritative: "My yes is yes, and my no is no. Neither will change."

There's a fine line between authoritarianism and permissiveness in teaching. But there is a winning play that works every time. It's the authoritative way.

It's not your job to control students, nor is it your job to rescue them. Teachers with authoritarian or permissive classroom management styles both use control in their attempts to ensure their students' success. Authoritarian teachers use control so their students will not have the opportunity to act up. Permissive teachers use control to smooth out the ripples of consequences before they could possibly reach the students. Both management styles rob students of the ability to make choices and then experience the beneficial or detrimental consequences now, rather than later in life with much higher stakes.

Authoritarian and permissive management styles also teach something beyond academics. Students learn that supposed rules can change. Here's the kicker. If established boundaries for classroom behavior can change, nothing in the classroom is really safe.

Authoritative teachers are in healthy authority over their classroom. They know that children crave boundaries and rules because such are a safety net. As a result, students know what to expect at all times.

> There is a winning play that works every time. It's the authoritative way.

54

If a student does X behavior, then he or she can expect that X will happen as a result each and every time. The game plan does not change. Everyone in the classroom follows the same rules and adheres to the same boundaries for behavior. Such an environment promotes learning, is based on mutual respect, and develops a relational connection between teacher and student.

Consequences for off-task behaviors are not an over-the-top attempt to prove a point or a lashing-out-in-frustration reaction. Neither are they excused. They merely flow as natural consequences of the undesired behavior. When you allow natural consequences to reign, what smarts for a moment becomes a smart life lesson.

Establishing Your Classroom's Tone

What atmosphere do you want to cultivate in your classroom? What adjectives would you use to describe that atmosphere? Perhaps, *positive, caring, supportive, invigorating, challenging, safe, respectful,* and *encouraging*?

The minute you step into the classroom, you are empowered as the authority. Authoritarian, permissive, and authoritative teaching styles all play out in different ways in the

> When you allow natural consequences to reign, what smarts for a moment becomes a smart life lesson.

classroom, contributing to different tones. As you read them, ask yourself, *If I were a student, whose classroom would I rather call home for this school year?*

Authoritarian teachers loom large and in charge. Their high need for control and respect can come off to students as dictatorial and uncaring. Informing students what they will do and when they will do it without a relational connection appears cold and unsupportive.

Students interpret this as the teacher saying, "It's either my way or the hallway…right to the principal's office. You will follow all my rules because I'm an adult and your teacher, and therefore I know best. I don't care if you like it or not. Especially because I don't really expect you to behave. So, I'm saying it upfront: if you don't follow my rules, you'll pay…dearly."

Dictator-type classrooms produce fearful, unmotivated, and rebellious students. Anxiety runs high, and competition between students intensifies. Students interpret the lack of teacher support as, "I don't like you very much. You're a bother, and I don't think you'll ever turn out to be anything. You're just who I'm stuck with this year."

Kids pick up fast on how you feel about them. Do you see them as interesting individuals? People you look forward to knowing? Or are they only the next batch of cows in the new school year's cattle car? Using the authoritarian style misses the 3 Rs. Students may learn from their textbooks, but they're learning something else more: what *not to do* in relationships.

Permissive teachers love their students and go out of their way to make sure each student feels loved and appreciated. Such a focus initially helps in the launch of the student-teacher relationship. However, it often goes downhill from there. The teacher may be ill-prepared for the lesson. Not much time is spent on-task, so academic learning is minimal. Students are not required to think before the teacher rescues them by providing the answer. There is little discipline and follow-through, so negative behavior spreads.

What does the permissive style say to students? "I really don't have a clue how to run a classroom. Can somebody help me? Anybody? Would someone else volunteer to be in charge?" Again, more enterprising students would be happy to jump into that gap, and classroom chaos will ensue.

The showers of love and appreciation wear thin as students realize what the lack of support is really saying: "I don't know what to do with you. Can't we all be friends and get through the year? Try to learn something along the way? You know I love you, right?" Classrooms with no rules or changing-with-the-daily-winds rules prompt insecurity, frustration, and a negative environment with no accountability. Such a style leads to rebellion and anger, since nothing permissive teachers say can be trusted.

To Ponder...

Consider this quote by Haim Ginott:

"I've come to the frightening conclusion that
I am the decisive element in the classroom.
It is my personal approach that creates the climate;
it's my daily mood that makes the weather.
I possess tremendous power
to make life miserable or joyous.
I can be a tool of torture
or an instrument of inspiration.
I can humiliate or humor, hurt or heal.
In all situations, it is my response that decides
whether a crisis is escalated or de-escalated,
and a person is humanized or de-humanized."[5]

Did you notice the words *I, me,* and *my?*
The atmosphere of your classroom starts
and ends with you.
What you do talks so loudly
that it trumps what you say every time.
Students look to you, their role model,
for inspiration and how to behave.

No one doubts that *authoritative* teachers are in charge of the classroom. They don't give that authority away easily, either. Unless the issue is a critical one of safety and security for the class and school, such teachers do their utmost to handle any issue within the classroom. Only as a last resort, after exhausting all other avenues, do they hand the child off to administrators for discipline.

Their ability to control and direct the orchestra with utmost confidence says to students, "I know what I'm doing. You can rest easy, knowing that I will do what I say I will do. This is a safe space for all. I am committed to keeping it that way." A teacher with such a perspective and an authoritative management style will work hard to be proactive in planning and preparing materials. He will ensure that students are clear on classroom expectations and can easily verbalize them.

Every student also is supported academically and emotionally. The teacher's every speech and action is based on well-thought-out principles, the view of students as learners, and an emphasis on getting to know each student individually. Every student gets the message loud and clear: "I'm glad you're in my class. I believe the best of you and expect the best. I'm committed to you achieving your personal best this year, and I'll do whatever I can to assist you in making that happen. We're on this journey together. I care about you. I look forward to getting to know you and finding out what makes you so unique. So, let's get to work!"

What Healthy Authority Looks Like

The beginning of a school year is an exhausting time for all teachers. You probably feel like you are drinking from a fire hydrant. There are not enough hours in the day to accomplish all you have to do. You are carefully scripting detailed lessons for the first days of school. You are focusing on creating a community of learners while cementing procedures, crafting routines, and establishing your authority.

When I was teaching in the early weeks of kindergarten, I'd come home and often fall asleep on the couch before dinnertime. It took every ounce of energy, tenacity, and creativity I had to create a community in my classroom with a group of five-year-olds.

I could have taken shortcuts. But I knew doing so would never work. If I stuck to my plan, the investment of my time and energy would pay off huge dividends.

Depending on the composition of students in a particular class, it sometimes took a few weeks to get the train moving smoothly down the kindergarten track. However, once the train gained momentum, it wasn't easy for it to be stopped or derailed. That's because the track had solidly been laid under that train.

That's not to say we didn't have some surprises once in a while. But we were able to handle them with respect for the individual child and the community of our classroom. Following is only one of many examples.

Maya decided to try out spitting on her classmates during recess. This was not acceptable or respectful behavior, so we spoke briefly. Maya missed the remainder of her recess outside during our conversation. I considered the lesson learned.

Not so. Maya decided to spit again the following day at recess. She sat out again, but this time the stakes were higher. I knew her mom would pick her up after school, so I quickly messaged her to come 10 minutes later. I wanted to talk with her after all the other students had been picked up.

That mom graciously agreed and showed up right on time. As the mid-day temperature easily reached almost 100 degrees, I stood on the sidewalk next to Maya and looked Mom in the eye.

I spoke only these words: "Your daughter has something to tell you."

What happened next was extraordinary. Maya wouldn't speak. Not a word.

Mom cajoled her.

Not a word.

Mom pleaded for an explanation of what had happened. Not a word.

Silence reigned. Finally, Maya broke down. She told her mom she had spit on her classmates at recess not only today but yesterday too.

That clearly startled mom handled the situation like a pro. She thanked her daughter for telling her the truth and said she was disappointed in her actions. Then she turned to me and said, "We'll talk this over tonight. Rest assured, it won't happen again."

She was right. The issue was over. No more spitting from Maya. On top of that, from that day forward Maya was respectful to her classmates in the classroom, in the hallways, and on the playground.

Issues can often be swiftly resolved through using actions and only the words necessary to serve the ball of responsibility into the court where it belongs. All the while you remain in healthy authority over that child and over your classroom. Such authority allows you to develop a relationship of trust with that child's guardian who sees your desire for a beneficial, learning outcome as issues crop up.

Students thrive in safe, conducive-to-learning environments where they have positive relationships with authoritative teachers. Before you set expectations or rules for your classroom, ask yourself: *Am I making these rules for my own convenience? Or because they have a real impact on my students' learning and establish a safe environment for all?*

Your view of your students makes all the difference. Instead of viewing them as children who should be molded in the ways in which you think they should go, view them first and foremost as *learners*. Learning will look different for each child. Where you can assist most is in helping each child discover how he or she learns the best.

If we could pick only two words to describe teachers who are in healthy authority over their classroom, it would be these: they "get it." Teachers who get it have a commonsense approach in all they do in the classroom. They make intentional choices that benefit their classroom culture and student outcomes. They are purposeful. They don't waste time. They build strong relationships with their students, families, and colleagues. They are confident in their skills. What they don't know, they actively seek to find out. They have a high bar of achievement that they are proud of.

> If we could pick only two words to describe teachers who are in healthy authority over their classroom, it would be these: they "get it."

They are also receptive to new ideas and eager to try them out. They observe others to find out the story behind the story. They curb gut reactions to behaviors because of their keen observation skills. As a result, they don't suffer from open-mouth-insert-foot syndrome. Instead they give themselves time to choose how they will respond.

They are in healthy authority over their classrooms, and that authority plays out in their teaching style. They manage their classroom as masterfully as a concert master conducts an orchestra. They have high, positive expectations for their students and hold those students accountable for their actions with real-life consequences. They promote self-control through encouraging the formation of good habits, a hard work ethic, and the ability to focus on the task at hand.

Their classrooms are safe spaces. Students know what to expect because the rules apply to all and don't change. Authoritative teachers mean what they say, say what they mean, and back up their words with action. They take a proactive approach, solving problems before they start.

Such teachers are also highly relational, going out of their way to connect uniquely with each student. They are fully aware of their students, including their expressions and responses, and what is going on in all parts of the classroom at all times. Teachers who get it observe how individual students operate in order to spur them on to achieve their personal bests.

When you get it, you arrange every area in the classroom so that it is visible to you. This line of sight means you are able to see the whole room at the same time. You are always monitoring students as they work.

In fact, you can divide a class into multiple groups that are doing different tasks and still maintain control of the students in every group and the class as a whole. You become, in effect, the all-seeing eye of every behavior. Such an approach allows you to curb off-task behaviors but also give nods of approvals and thumbs-ups to on-task behaviors. You notice and affirm a student who busily works on an assignment. You ask thought-provoking questions and call on non-volunteers as well as those with waving hands to increase engagement in the classroom.

Because you have an eagle-eye on your students' expressions, you know when to speed up or slow down on presenting the topic at hand. You are also able to catch a single student engaged in off-task behavior and swoop in using proximity or a disapproving look before the rest of the class is aware of any issue. Proximity is an amazingly simple tool. It can stop an offender in his tracks. It conveys a clear message: *I see you. I care about what you are doing. And if you proceed with doing that, I will hold you accountable.*

Best of all, that entire message is delivered without you saying a word. There's no interruption of the lesson. No rise of your blood pressure. No tightening of the vocal chords from pontificating. Truly, it's a magical act at its finest for teachers who get it.

Sure, you can deal with misconduct when it happens, and it will happen. Children are only human. But what if you could prevent it from happening in the first place? Now *there's* the ticket.

Authoritative teachers are masters at stopping distractions *before* they start. It is about being proactive, anticipating issues, and responding instead of reacting. In my growing-up years I used to swear that a couple of my teachers literally had eyes in the back of their heads. They just *knew* when any student, particularly me, was even *thinking* of goofing off. Before we could launch into trouble, they nipped the contemplation of mischief in the bud with a mere glance. I called it "The Look." You know exactly what I mean, don't you?

After a while, little Kevin Leman got really smart. I would cause trouble in *other* teachers' classes, but not *those* teachers. I knew they were in charge of the classroom. The classroom was run in an organized way, and the roadmap for each day was clear. They had high expectations, but I wanted to rise to those expectations. I might have been a hooligan sometimes, but those teachers treated me with respect, and, yes, sometimes with amusement, which made this lastborn as happy as a team mascot performing for a crowd. They were proactive in how they managed their classroom, in how they related to me, and in winning their students' active participation in learning.

> Stopping distractions *before* they start...is about being proactive, anticipating issues, and responding instead of reacting.

Taking the Proactive Approach in Classroom Management

Classroom management is the set of skills a teacher needs to plan, organize, and maintain a productive learning environment.

It allows for students to be taught independent decision-making so they assume increased responsibility for their own learning.

Setting the environment for a successfully managed classroom requires five proactive aspects: providing a roadmap, managing physical space, managing time, and managing materials in a way that ensures learning objects are reached and students are actively participating. They aren't something you do one time in the first week of school. They are all-day affairs every day you teach.

Providing a Roadmap

The beginning of the school year is a critical time for teachers in establishing their authority and providing a roadmap. What are you going to accomplish this year? And how are you going to do that? You need to know, but so do your students. If they don't have a roadmap, chaos will reign.

Have you established hallway and bathroom behaviors? What about stipulating desired behaviors at lunch and recess?

Have you trained your students in classroom volume level? Enough for the class to hear your responses but no shouting allowed?

> If they don't have a roadmap, chaos will reign.

Do your students know how to enter classrooms, including art, music, and PE, that are outside of your home room?

Do they know the etiquette of asking and answering questions?

What nonverbal signals and verbal signals do you use to call the class to attention? For example, an effective verbal signal before starting a new subject could be this:

Teacher: "All set?"
Students say in unison: "You bet!"

An effective nonverbal signal to transition from small-group discussion back to the class as a group could be a hand raised by the teacher. Here's how it works. Students see the teacher's hand uplifted as she walks around the class. They stop discussing and lift their own hand until the entire class is quiet.

Developing and routinely using such signals sends simultaneous messages to your students. First, you are in charge of your classroom and always adhere to the roadmap you provided for the students. Students don't have to second-guess your intentions. Second, each lesson is important, urgent, and worth the time you will spend on it as a group. Therefore each lesson has a set start time and end time. Nothing and no one will distract from the learning.

Whether your school year is starting or already in full swing, there's no time like the present to establish roadmaps.

Managing Your Physical Space

How you arrange your classroom and how you move about that classroom says far more about how you view students than you might think. Are desks and tables arranged in straight rows or in pods? Rows indicate that you believe students learn best on their own, in cookie-cutter fashion. Pods optimize learning, discussion, and collaboration.

An Apple a Day

Allowing students to choose their own seats is a common rookie mistake. Don't fall for trying to make them happy or attempting to be their new best friend by allowing them to sit with their friends. You are in charge of your room, and students will work best in a seating arrangement you create. They might learn a thing or two about relating to others and make some new friends.

Sure, you'll have to modify the seating chart from time to time as issues crop up. Some students are like oil and water. They don't mix well. But your creation of that chart contributes to the overall message you must send as the teacher: *you* are the authority and are in healthy control of the classroom.

Where you place your desk also says a lot about you as a teacher and what is most important to you. Do you place it at the front of the room, with a carpet or rug between you and your students? At the back of the room, with floor space between you and your students? Or in the center or side of the room, with the class surrounding you?

If your desk is front and center in the room, it sends the message that you are highly rule-oriented. You face every student head-on, so you can keep your eagle-eye on them. You are more likely to be an authoritarian teacher who feels most comfortable with a clear division between teacher and student. Or you are a newbie teacher who has been told in school that's where your desk should be, and you haven't yet questioned that idea.

Your desk being at the back of the room can connote several ideas. You might be seen as a teacher who is not confident and would rather blend into the woodwork. You might be seen as taking a backseat, with your students running their own stage show. Or you might be seen as the teacher who expects the worst of her students, so she wants to keep an eye on them from the back to catch them being bad.

> Where you place your desk says a lot about you as a teacher and what is most important to you.

If your desk is in the side or center of the room, it sends the message that you are part of the group but also the one in charge of providing the learning. You are the all-seeing eye and presence. Nothing in the classroom goes on outside your sphere of awareness.

How you move about the classroom makes a great impact too. Using whiteboards, smartboards, document cameras, computer, or projectors in small doses can be helpful. Used too much, they tether teachers to the front of the classroom. A teacher who remains stationary and plugged-in to devices invites behavior issues throughout the room. When teachers are too stationary, students who think they can't be seen will play at their desk, chat with a neighbor, or engage in myriad off-task behaviors.

Masterful teachers circle the room. They use proximity as the first line of defense in classroom management. They make eye contact with students who are off-task, gently and quietly removing a distraction with no fanfare. They redirect a student who is not paying attention by passing close to that desk and stopping briefly. Since students never know where the teacher is going to move next, they're more likely to pay attention and stay on task.

To Ponder...

The mind is not a vessel to be filled,
but a fire to be kindled.

PLUTARCH

How will you kindle the imagination of your class and spur their learning? Certainly not by pouring all of your knowledge into their heads but by allowing students to wrestle with ideas, facts, information, and develop their own conclusions. Remember: your role is to help your students *learn how to think*, not to do the thinking for them.

Educator Charlotte Mason once said, "What a child digs for becomes his own possession."[6] Teachers should function as the great facilitators of the classroom, combining the

> Your role is to help your students *learn how to think,* not to do the thinking for them.

arrangement of physical space, keeping in close proximity to students, and staying on the move to create an environment conducive to energetic learning.

Plan your classroom space accordingly. If it's time to rearrange your physical space, do so. There's nothing like a little rearrangement to send the message, *Things are going to be different around here, in a good way.* Don't explain yourself. Just do it. Let your students come in the next day, see the new arrangement, and find their seats. Let them wonder why you did it. A little intrigue is good for the classroom.

Simply wait for that teachable moment, when the students themselves do the asking so they're open to really hearing and processing what you say. (Hint: this works well with *all* children, including teens.) Lest you doubt, that time will come. Kids are innately curious. One of the more brave students will ask, "Uh, Teacher, why did you move our desks?" Then you will have the opportunity to briefly explain your view of your role as teacher and theirs to be responsible for their own learning. It's also a good time to provide the roadmap and institute other changes discussed in this chapter.

You have nothing to lose, and everything to gain. So do your students.

Managing Your Time

If you've ever said, "There simply isn't enough time to do everything I need to do in a day!" then join the club. It is the biggest complaint of teachers.

Granted, teachers do have a lot of responsibilities. But each of us has the same amount of time packed into a school day. The question isn't, "How much time do I have?" It is, "How will

I choose to spend that time?" Some successful ways to manage time are as follows.

Provide a roadmap and verbal or nonverbal signals for your students. We noted these previously, but they're worth noting again for a simple reason. If you make improvements in *any* area of teaching, you'll automatically boost your success in other areas of teaching. A roadmap and signals help you avoid the time-wasters of explaining transitions in the school day. Instead lessons and activities flow from one to the other with simple signals or fun competition. You might say, "Yesterday it took us 23 seconds to get ready for math. Let's see if we can beat that time today. Ready, go!" Such strategies avoid the majority of student distractions and the potential for complaints. They also assist in promoting the view of the class as a group that works, plays, and stays together.

Refine your organizational skills. To optimize the time you do have, prepare a well-written lesson plan with objectives in advance (more on that to come in this chapter). Post the day's schedule on the board for you and your students. Not only will it help you keep on track, but your firstborn or only born students will appreciate knowing what the day holds for them as well. Taking a minute or two to post that schedule at the start of every school day also affirms your position of authority and confirms that you respect your students' time. They know you have a game plan and will stick to it.

> The question isn't, "How much time do I have?" It is, "How will I choose to spend that time?"

Compile a single master document of your curriculum for the school year. As you teach your lessons, if you discover that your estimate is off regarding how long a specific lesson will take to teach or a group project to complete, update that master plan. Do it the first break you have in a quiet classroom. It might feel like an inconvenience now, but you'll thank yourself in a year when you teach that lesson again.

Use your downtime wisely. When your class is out of the classroom, what do you do? Do you organize your materials so you can jump immediately into the next subject without losing traction? Do you work on the following day's schedule and prepare those materials?

It might be tempting to take a long break in the teacher's lounge with a cup of coffee or a sugar-inspired treat, but look at it this way. The more time you spend in that lounge, the more work you'll need to take home with you. Instead, discipline yourself to be as productive as you can in the hours that you are in the school building. Keep your eye on the end goal: a free evening or an entire weekend. Wouldn't those both be nice?

Indicators of Ineffective Classroom Management

- The classroom feels cold and sterile, like a doctor's office.

- Students are stressed, fearful, and refuse to take risks to answer questions due to an authoritarian teaching style.

- The classroom is disorganized, lacks clear procedures, and feels like a free-for-all zone.

- A permissive teaching style puts students in charge by default.

- The teacher repeats directions and has to cajole or threaten to get things done.

- Students dilly-dally in starting activities. They only respond after the third warning.

- Students look bored, tuned out, and talk to neighbors while the lesson is being taught.

- The teacher can't complete the lesson since time is spent managing the class.

- The teacher addresses the group as a whole, rather than connecting with individuals.

Indicators of Effective Classroom Management

- The classroom has a warm, energetic, positive, organized feeling.

- The teacher demonstrates an authoritative style, with healthy control and support, in a conducive-to-learning environment.

- The teacher provides a roadmap, gives clear directions once, and students are expected to comply.

- Students respond immediately to teacher signals and requests.

- The teacher manages the class effectively using tone of voice and a varied volume.

- The teacher uses verbal or nonverbal signals to transition from one activity to the next.

- Students are engaged and excited about learning.

- The teacher completes the lesson due to proactive management of the room, time, and materials.

- The teacher is consistent, compassionate, and seeks to authentically connect with each student.

Managing Your Materials

It's vital to have everything you need for classes at your fingertips at the beginning of the day. That means *prior* to your students entering your classroom.

Think of it this way. Many children have the attention of a gnat. Turn your back on them for a minute and you invite them to turn, talk, and engage in off-task behavior. Yes, you're busy. And occasionally you will forget something. You are, after all, human. Use those occurrences as a teachable moment for the class.

"For our next activity, we'll need a (you list the item)," you say. "But I don't have that item right here. Do you know why? This morning I allowed myself to be distracted. I did not put that item where it should go. (You point to the subject bin.) While I walk to the file cabinet at the back of the room to get it, let's brainstorm. What ideas do you have for how I might better remember an item like that tomorrow?"

While retrieving the item, you call on students to contribute ideas. After the item is retrieved, you thank the class for their ideas, helpfulness, and attention. Then you move directly into the lesson. The way you have handled that distraction is in itself a microcosm lesson for students. They realize that adults aren't perfect, can make mistakes, and that problems can result. But when adults admit their mistakes, seek to correct them with a positive attitude and brainstorming, problems can be addressed. Life can move on.

> Many children have the attention of a gnat. Turn your back on them for a minute and you invite them to turn, talk, and engage in off-task behavior.

Healthy adults admit when they blow it, and they seek to change how they do things. You didn't plan to be distracted, but you might as well use the result of it as a teachable moment. Doing so is to your students' and your own benefit, since you're more likely now to check that list twice for materials tomorrow.

Classroom management is not, as we said earlier, a one-time occurrence. It's all day, every day. Masterful teachers use the growing cache of tools in their toolbelt and are eager to procure more to manage their classroom. They are authoritative. They establish a positive, caring, supportive, invigorating, challenging, safe, respectful, and encouraging tone up front.

They place their desk smack-dab in the middle of the action so they have close proximity to the students at all times. They are the hub of the wheel of learning that takes place. However, students are also regarded as important spokes, responsible for their own learning. Student desks are placed in pods to encourage discussion and collaboration in partners or small groups under the teacher's watchful eye.

Masterful teachers give clear, simple instructions and a roadmap for the day. They use verbal and nonverbal cues that are understood by the entire class. Such cues are used for transitions, to move the learning forward, and to cement the view that every lesson is important and deserves the time allotted to it. Such teachers are organized in regard to material management, making the most of their prep time and class time.

Being prepared with an organizational system in place is vital to your success in the classroom. To do so, you need to be able to write powerful learning objectives and craft active participation strategies that will keep all your students engaged in learning.

LEMANISM #8

To get somewhere, you need a game plan
and a set destination.

Writing Powerful Learning Objectives

What is an *objective*? Simply stated, it is change or motion toward a goal with overt actions. An objective has four parts. It gives a condition, describes the type of learning, the overt behavior that results, and the expected performance level. Here is an example of a powerfully written learning objective:

> "Given 10 sentences with examples of figurative language, students will demonstrate an understanding of the difference in similes and metaphors by circling metaphors and underlining similes with 85 percent accuracy."

Let's break it into its specific parts:

Condition: Given 10 sentences with examples of figurative language, students will…
Learning: …demonstrate an understanding of the difference in similes and metaphors…
Behavior: …by circling metaphors and underlining similes…
Performance Level: …with 85 percent accuracy.

The 4 Parts of Learning Objectives
• Condition
• Learning
• Behavior
• Performance Level

Learning objectives also need to follow the "4 Ms." They must be **M**ade first, **M**anageable, **M**easurable, and **M**ost important.

Made first: Objectives are formulated before your lesson. They cannot be an afterthought. They should guide your lesson and activity and clearly indicate what the student should be able to do by the end of the lesson. Choose a learning objective that aligns to a state standard, and be sure all students understand the academic vocabulary in the objective. Unpacking the objective is necessary to ensure all students can verbalize what the objective is and what they are expected to do.

Manageable: An objective can only be effective if you can teach it in a single lesson. To make larger skills manageable, break them into smaller steps. For example, "Students will understand the Pythagorean theorem" is a large skill and therefore an unmanageable objective. Try instead, "Students will write the formula for the Pythagorean theorem," a smaller step.

Measurable: Effective objectives can be measured. Avoid verbs such as *know, understand, learn, comprehend, appreciate, familiarize,* and *study.* These words are not measurable. The teacher must check for understanding after teaching the objective. One way to do this is through an "Exit Ticket." At the end of the lesson, students must demonstrate what they have learned. For example, "Students will write a descriptive paragraph that includes a topic sentence, three supporting detail sentences, and a closing sentence." That is a measurable goal.

Most important: Choose an objective that is best for your students' learning. Post it and review it prior to each lesson, and then assess it at the end of the lesson. It's an easy way to know whether you accomplished your purpose or whether you need to attack learning from a different method. Masterful teachers learn how to adapt their teaching methods based on the makeup of different classes. Just because a specific method worked for one school year doesn't mean it will work for next year's class.

The 4 Ms of Learning Objectives

- Made first

- Manageable

- Measurable

- Most important

What might a planned lesson look like? What format could you follow? Educator Madeline Hunter suggests breaking down the time you have for planning and teaching each lesson into percentages.[7]

Objective: 30%. By writing this before the lesson, you provide the roadmap for what the student should be able to do when the lesson is done.

Independent Practice: 10%. You give students the opportunity to further apply or practice using the new information.

Guided Practice: 10%. You carefully monitor to ensure students duplicate the skill, process, procedure, or exercise correctly.

Anticipatory Set: 10%. You hook the students into the new lesson by encouraging them to connect past information with the new information being presented.

Teach: 30%. This is the active time you spend conveying the new subject in order to achieve your objective.

Closure: 10%. You review the day's goal or objective and check for understanding. What did your students accomplish? What did they learn? You preview tomorrow's lesson and review today's assignment. Effective closure strategies include:

- What was the purpose of today's lesson?

- Write a brief description of what you learned today.

- Turn and tell your neighbor what you learned today.

- Write a test question based off our lesson today.

An Apple a Day

Pick a recent teaching objective you have written.

Rewrite it with the four specific parts of *Condition, Learning, Behavior,* and *Performance Level.*

Test your objective. Is it manageable and measurable?

Crafting Active Participation Strategies

Some teachers are happy if their students aren't falling asleep, aren't talking over the top of them, and appear somewhat to be paying attention to the lesson. But you don't have to settle for any of those as your best option. You can achieve active participation from "all of the students all of the time."

Active participation is the *consistent* engagement of the minds of all learners with the subject at hand. Ask yourself often during your teaching, *How many students are actively engaged right now?* How do you know? Your "get it" comes nicely into play. You observe their expressions, their body language, and their actions.

Typically, the larger the group, the lower the engagement. The smaller the group, the higher the engagement. Pause and think about that for a moment.

Go ahead. Ask your question. We know you're thinking it.

"You mean to say that when I'm teaching the whole class with those slides I worked so hard on for an entire weekend that, when I use them, participation and engagement are at their lowest?"

Yes, that's what we're saying. There's a better way, and you don't have to spend an entire weekend doing it. It's simple, in fact. You have to know what *doesn't* work and stop doing that. And you have to know what *does* work and give it a whirl as you go about your business in the classroom.

What doesn't work? The following common techniques impede and interfere with active participation. They don't prompt students to think through the content

> The larger the group, the lower the engagement. The smaller the group, the higher the engagement.

and justify their answers. Instead, they cause students to disengage with the content.

Whole group instruction. In the 1980s movie *Ferris Bueller's Day Off,* there's a classic what-not-to-do-as-a-teacher scene. The economics teacher is tethered to the front of the room lecturing, pointing to the blackboard behind him. He attempts to find anyone in the room who might know the right answer by repeating, "Anyone? Anyone?" Finally he gives up and answers his own questions. There is zero percent engagement with the class. The students are clearly bored: falling asleep on their desks, blowing bubbles with their gum, and their gazes are totally out to lunch. Talk about an exercise in educational futility.

Trying to teach the whole group simultaneously is a sure-fire way to lose student engagement. That's because they have stopped caring about the content, the class, or the teacher. No one is paying attention because they are not required to do so. All students are disengaged. Some will be distracting others. Some will be sportin' a 'tude. But none will be learning.

Students will be highly engaged if they are doing activities such as hands-on science labs or are a part of a small group working on a specific task. These tasks are inherently worthwhile, meaningful, and enjoyable. This type of engagement is particularly true if teachers have close oversight, high expectations, and high accountability. Without close teacher monitoring, students might be well behaved, not causing any fuss in class, and look like they're complying with the activity. However, they're not really engaged in the learning process because the teacher doesn't require it of them.

Round-robin or popcorn reading. Both are widely accepted ways for students to read content aloud. The only real difference in the two is that, in round-robin reading, there is a set order in which the students will read aloud. In popcorn reading, there is no set order. How do they work? The teacher calls on students to read a few sentences, a paragraph, or a page aloud. It may seem like participation, but it is really forced, uncomfortable participation.

For poor readers, self-conscious students, or students with anxiety, reading aloud can be a real struggle. Instead of paying attention to the content being read, they're spending the time counting the paragraphs ahead in round robin to see what they might have to read. In popcorn reading, students are thinking, *This would be a great time to use the restroom.* Often students doing the reading feel a great tension and then a relief of *Oh, good, I'm off the hook for the day* when their turn is over. They tend to then sit back and wait for the lesson to end rather than paying attention to the content.

Asking rhetorical, open-ended, targeted, or robotic questions. Rhetorical questions can be confusing. Students wonder, *Do I answer? Do I not answer? Is this really a question?* Rhetorical questions don't generate answers because no answer is really expected. For example, you're teaching history, and you say, "Now, what does this mean for this period of history? It means that we should learn from history so we don't make the same mistakes." Such rhetoric is not only tiresome to say but boring to your students.

Nothing puts a class to sleep faster than rhetorical questions. They don't promote the awe and wonder that should come as part and parcel with learning in the classroom. If something is commonsense and not worth saying, why take precious class time to say it at all?

Open-ended questions such as, "Who would like to…?" invite students to disengage. Every student is silently answering, *Nuh-uh, no thanks. I don't want to do that.* The result is that the class as a whole sits in silence. Asking, "What do you think about this time period?" without identifying a specific area you would like students to comment on will understandably generate blank stares. They have no idea what answer you are fishing for. If the style of questions makes student learning optional, who wouldn't check out and go on a mind vacation?

> If the style of questions makes student learning optional, who wouldn't check out and go on a mind vacation?

Targeted questions use a student's name at the beginning of a question. Problem is, as soon as a name is announced, the rest of the class shuts down. They know they're off the hook…at least for this question. Teachers also tend to use targeted questions as a "gotcha!" strategy. Suddenly the teacher calls out the name of a student who clearly is not paying attention in hopes of swiftly redirecting his behavior. Such questions will always backfire since they create tension and mistrust in the classroom and break down the potential for any beneficial relationship with that student.

Robotic questions are ones like these: "Page 12 talked about the Russian Revolution. What did it say?" A robot could answer that question. Your student doesn't need to.

Always calling on students who raise their hands to answer. All teachers have one or two "pick me" students who constantly have their hands up to answer questions. But what about the other 20+ in the class? The ones who don't raise their hands? Who say, "Uh, I didn't raise my hand" if you do call on them? Calling only on volunteers throughout the lesson decreases engagement in the class as a whole. It takes students off the hook for their own learning.

What *does* work? Small tweaks in planning and execution can make a huge difference in capturing the engagement of the entire class. Why not try one or more of the following ideas this week?

Vary your voice. One of the most effective tools you can use in class to encourage active participation is your voice. Yes, you read that right. Think of it this way. If you had to listen to someone drone on in a monotone, it's likely your attention would wander. After all, it's clear the speaker himself lacks energy and enthusiasm for the subject matter, so why should you listen? And if you hear someone who constantly talks loudly, you might tend to tune them out to save your eardrums.

If you really want your students to listen, lower your voice to just above a whisper. Try it! See what happens. It's actually one of the more effective classroom techniques a teacher can use.

Your class responds to the environment you are creating. If you are loud, expect your class to be loud. If you are calm and soft, your class will meet those expectations.

> If you really want your students to listen, lower your voice to just above a whisper.

Masterful teachers learn how to vary their voices. They know their voice is a tool and they use it smartly. They show excitement. They smile and nod. They give straightforward instructions in a no-nonsense tone. They provide information in a compelling way that makes students lean forward and listen.

"Did you know that snakes have designs on their bodies that protect them from predators?" the teacher says.

A student raises her hand. "You mean, like a tattoo?"

The teacher laughs. "That's a great analogy. Yes, they actually look like tattoos. Let's take a look at some and figure out why you think they're patterned like that."

Vary your teaching techniques. When you do have to teach the whole group, change up your teaching techniques. You'll be less predictable, so students are more likely to pay attention and also anticipate what could come next. A writing teacher I know once dumped an entire trash can of crumpled paper over his head to demonstrate how many drafts he had to write of a paper before he finally had a readable draft. It was two o'clock in the afternoon, and his students were sleepy and not paying attention. You wanna bet they will remember that lesson decades later?

Pull your chair up to smaller groups of students one at a time. Discuss various aspects of the subject together. Reteach any components that don't seem clear to that particular group of students. Assembling students in smaller groups multiple times a day will assist with active participation and give you real-time feedback on students' understanding. You can differentiate instruction for the various groups and more effectively meet the needs of all your students.

Use movement to your advantage. If you notice that a student isn't paying attention, don't publicly call him out on it. Instead move closer in proximity to that student. Catch his eye. Let him know you are aware he isn't engaged. Sometimes that's all it takes to get a student back on track. Start with private discipline as much as possible, and you'll build your relational connection with that student.

Constantly monitor your students. Get up. Walk around. Listen to small-group conversations. Toss in a new question.

Be adaptable to the class and the day. Let's say you teach first grade. You know your first graders are adjusting to a longer school session. Why not take them to the playground to teach math? Use a ball that bounces from child to child as you

> Get up. Walk around. Listen to small-group conversations. Toss in a new question or two.

say together: "1 + 1 = 2. 2 + 2 = 4. 3 + 3 = 6." And so on. It's an active, happy way to learn addition for students who struggle with the concept of math.

Prepare questions in advance. Write out and plan your questions for each lesson carefully in advance. Student outcomes increase when you are purposeful about the questions you want to ask.

Get the whole class involved in answering questions. Create the expectation in your room that you can call on anyone at any time. Call on the enthusiastic hand-raisers sometimes. But address the non-volunteers 70 percent of the time. Do it with gentleness for the timid ones. A simple preface of, "One of you in this room has showed great interest in this subject. In fact, I'd love to hear what he thinks about the question. Timothy, would you tell us what you think about (and you phrase the question)?"

Why do it that way? Because here's a secret: your students want to please you. They want to belong to the class. They want to make a contribution. They sometimes don't know how or haven't worked up the courage to start the process themselves.

If Timothy has difficulty forming his answer, sum it up after he is done with, "What I think I hear you saying is…." Then ask him a related follow-up question. Doing this will not only show him your interest in what he thinks but also encourage him to clarify or justify his answer. Having students explain what they're learning is a phenomenal learning technique. What we figure out for ourselves tends to stick with us.

Vary the ways and times you ask questions. Train your students to ask questions of each other using the Socratic method. Then split them into small groups to try it out. Such a method fosters critical thinking, enhances the ability to explain ideas as they develop, and encourages deeper relationships and understanding of unique perspectives.

> Here's a secret.
> Your students
> want to please you.
> They want to
> belong to the class.
> They want to
> make a contribution.

You may choose to make certain days, assignments, lessons, or discussion "no raised hands needed" times. At those times all students are on the hot seat, with participation a requirement. Students must be responsible to participate in their own learning. They need to understand that they are not in your class simply to fill space. They are there to actively engage in the content. Therefore, participation is not an option. It is part and parcel of the standard curriculum.

Calling on all students comes with an important responsibility for teachers. All students must be encouraged to share their points of view, opinions, and beliefs in a respectful way. The classroom must be a safe place for students to be who they are, to be respected for their opinions despite others' disagreement, and to be accepted as part of the group.

Ask invigorating questions that promote active participation. Instead of *what* questions that simply test recall and memorization, ask *how* and *why* questions. These are higher-level questions that test what your students are observing and learning. They also assist students in connecting new concepts with previous learning. *How* and *why* questions invite your students into pondering answers. They involve excitement, strategy, and imagination.

For example, "If you lived during this time of history and had all the power in the world, what one thing would you do differently, and why?" Your students won't forget that question after your lesson is over. Their answers might generate invigorating discussion at home that night too.

Use wait time to boost learning potential. How long should you wait for student response after asking a question? And how long should you wait after a student gives an answer for them to clarify their answer or add more to their answer?

The average teacher rarely waits more than one and a half seconds after asking students a question. Then, only half a second later, that teacher calls on a specific student. Additionally, after a student answers a question, the teacher immediately asks another, leaving no room for discussion, explanation, or follow-up questions from other students. Did you know that by doubling that uninterrupted wait time to only three seconds, there are tremendous benefits in learning?[8]

> The average teacher rarely waits more than one and a half seconds after asking students a question.

Studies show that waiting three seconds positively influenced the length and correctness of students' responses.[9] The "I don't know" responses decreased. Students volunteering to answer increased. Test scores increased.

There were benefits for teachers too. Their questioning strategies became more varied and more flexible. The quality of their questions increased. The quantity of their questions decreased. They asked questions that were more complex and required higher-level thinking.

It's been said that patience is a virtue.[10] It is, and it is hard to employ it at times, especially for some of us with plow-ahead personalities. But patience in teaching works.

The next time there's silence in the classroom after you ask a question, don't jump in and rephrase the question. Don't ask another question or answer the question yourself. Let the blissful silence reign. Allow students uninterrupted time to process and think. Allow them time to lead in answering that question.

Moving too quickly through a series of questions and information can leave some students in the dust. We don't all learn through the same methods or process information the same way or at the same speed. That's why it's vital that your wait-and-think time is long and purposeful.

Some students will quickly process an answer and be ready to share. Still other students need time to process the question first before formulating their answer. Too quick of a pace negates the chance for these students to process what you're asking. Other students will deeply dissect the question to determine the root of what you're really asking or will automatically think of multiple layers to an answer. That makes any no or yes questions difficult to answer. The answers that come swiftly may not always be the most meaningful ones from which the whole class could benefit.

There's another benefit to waiting. You show your students respect by allowing them to wrestle with the subject matter and come up with answers themselves. That gift assists them in generating confidence in their ability to problem-solve. Now that's a gift that will keep on giving, and giving, and giving.

LEMANISM #9
Never do for a student
what he can do for himself.

How can you improve your wait time to produce such stellar results? Simply be aware of your own wait time. Count three to five seconds in your head until adequate, uninterrupted think time becomes a habit. Partner that strategy of wait time with getting the whole class involved by breaking into small groups or sharing answers with partners. Hold all students responsible for their own learning, and your entire class will be actively engaged. As a bonus, they'll be listening to their peers' opinions and answers and refining their own as they learn alongside each other.

Never fear silence in the classroom. Wait time isn't dead time. It's learning time.

Using Behaviors to Your Advantage

You are beginning a lesson and want to find out what students already know. How might you assess their prior knowledge? You can do so by using both observable and non-observable behaviors as a strategy to gauge the level of active participation.

> Never fear silence in the classroom. Wait time isn't dead time. It's learning time.

Some behaviors such as imagining, thinking, picturing, remembering, visualizing, reflecting, and pondering are not observable. That means it's harder to know if students are actually participating in them. However, if used correctly, such behaviors have the ability to make students think. They may also appeal particularly to the learning styles of introspective and artistic children. They present the opportunity to wrestle with information, make connections to prior knowledge, ask questions, follow the rabbit trail a while, and draw a conclusion or two.

Other student behaviors are both observable and measurable. These include writing, explaining what they learned to a partner, summarizing a topic for the group, drawing a picture, role-playing, answering on magnetic boards, or demonstrating learning in any other observable way. At any given point in your lesson, you can scan the room and easily see which students are engaged. Those who are actively participating are drawing, talking, creating, or writing. They aren't sitting idle. They aren't passively allowing others to do the thinking for them. They are engaged with the information and doing something with it. These more active options may especially appeal to the learning styles of kinesthetic (motion) learners and children who tend to be more social.

Learning tends to stick for students who have to explain what they've learned, whether verbally or on paper. That's because students don't give rote, memorized answers. They must justify their answers based on what they've learned. This can occur between partners, in small groups, or in wait/think time after you ask a question.

An Apple a Day

Following are common classroom activities. Do you think they promote active participation? Why or why not?

If not, what would you do instead to increase student engagement?

Science: The teacher calls a student to the board to solve an equation.
Reading: A student reads aloud from their literature book as others follow along.
Math: The teacher poses a problem to the class and has students write their individual responses on paper.

Masterful teachers prompt their students to learn how to learn for themselves. After a student answers a question or explains what he or she has learned, the teacher then says, "I see. So, you're saying (and you reiterate what the student said). You have a good point. What do you think about (and you bring up another aspect)? And how are the two things connected?" This encourages active participation and next-step thinking not only for that student but for the class in general.

Remember: children will rise to your expectations of them.

The classroom is the place where students have the opportunity to take ownership over their own education. Through the rigorous education that you provide, they hopefully become individuals who can think for themselves, form and defend an argument, think critically, and apply reason. That's why teaching is such a highly honorable, high-stakes occupation.

> The classroom is the place where students have the opportunity to take ownership over their own education.

Future leaders are seated in your classroom right now. You have the unfathomable opportunity this year to influence the next generation of leaders by making a positive impact on their lives. How will you train them up?

To Ponder...

Knowledge has to pass through the heart.
Teaching is personal.
Students will remember your lessons
when you connect them
to their own life experiences.

Successfully managing your classroom and yourself is critical to becoming a great teacher by Friday. We've covered a lot in this chapter, including establishing healthy authority, crafting your classroom tone, providing a roadmap, arranging your room to spur learning, tips for managing your time and materials wisely, and ideas for encouraging active participation. As you think about what excellence will look like in your classroom, you might want to reconsider each section one at a time. We hope it will be a chapter you return to, time and again, for inspiration when you need it most.

Now that we've established educational basics and managing your classroom, we turn next to your students. When there's a whole room of them and not enough of you or your time to go around, how can you create a relational classroom that also highlights learning? The next chapter will help you get behind your students' eyes. You'll find out what they need most and how you can uniquely help while building a classroom community where other students, teachers, and parents say, "Wow, I wish I were in her class."

Winning Play #3
Get Behind Each Student's Eyes

*Understanding kick-starts motivation,
creative problem-solving,
and builds classroom community.*

Some years ago I was teaching kindergarten in a classroom with polished cement floors. (Stay posted for why I mention the type of floors.) I had a class size of thirty-three wriggly five-year-olds and knew my management needed to be strong to effectively teach these young minds. We got past the first week with little or no issues as I set out to teach my classroom expectations, establish routines, and start to build relationships.

Among my students was a set of twins who were not only intelligent but kind. Isla, one of the twins, was having a difficult time beginning kindergarten despite her twin's presence in the room. I partnered with the home (more about this in Friday's chapter) and tried several strategies that I had successfully used before. We taped her family picture into her pencil box so she could "sneak and peek" whenever needed.

That worked for a few days, but Isla still struggled as we sat on the carpet for quiet or activity time and during lunch and recess because the picture was not with her. Tears would flow. She said she missed her mom and wanted her mom throughout the day.

Again I communicated with the home and tried other techniques to help ease Isla's mind. I sat her next to her twin and enlisted his help to encourage her with her kindergarten tasks. I partnered her with gentle classmates who showed concern about her. And I allowed her to draw pictures for her mom during the day as time allowed.

Still no progress. Again I conversed with her mom, who was wonderfully calm but also concerned. She told me she had recently purchased a small polished red stone heart that would fit into the palm of Isla's hand. She theorized that, if her daughter had the stone to hold, she might be able to think of her mom but squeeze the stone when she felt like crying. It might allow Isla to focus on schoolwork. "Would you be willing to try that approach?" the mom asked.

Of course I said yes. The stone came to school. Sure enough, Isla hung onto that little red heart for dear life. She brought it to the carpet when we transitioned there. It went with her to recess, lunch, art, music, and PE. Isla loved that heart and found great comfort in holding it. All was well in that kindergartener's world because of one little stone heart.

> All was well in that kindergartener's world because of one little stone heart.

Getting to that creative solution required the 3 Rs. I worked on my relationship with Isla. I conversed back and forth with her mother. I looped in her brother and classmates to help. That's why we say relationships are at the heart of teaching. Before you can craft learning techniques to match each student, you need to see the world through her eyes as a unique individual. Isla needed a reminder of her mother with her. Then she was able to move ahead into the wider world of school with a positive outlook that would allow her to achieve her personal best.

When you have so many students and limited time, how can you accomplish seeing the world through each of their eyes? Understanding the basics of birth order can help.

Birth Order Basics Revealed

Want to help your students grow in their relational connections and stretch their horizons? Put a firstborn and a lastborn right next to each other. There will be a lot of initial frustration because the two operate so differently, but they'll learn a great deal from each other. Put two firstborns next to each other, though, and they might spend most of their partner time determined to prove who's right and nitpicking over the assignment details.

Put two lastborns next to each other, and they'll be shooting the breeze instead of tackling that assignment. Ask, "How is your assignment coming?" and their response will likely be, "Uh, what assignment?" Then there are the middleborns, who are highly adjustable no matter their placement. Still, they might prefer another middleborn who understands where they are coming from. See how helpful knowing a bit about birth order can be in the classroom?

Following is a quick trip through the birth orders and what students of those birth orders need most from you.

If You're a Firstborn (or Only Child)

You are the rockstar, the oldest kid in your family. You talked first, walked first, and entered school first. You're either an only child or the role model for your younger siblings, but you don't feel all that special. You live constantly with pressure: your parents' eagle eyes on you, extra chores (you still don't understand why your little sister can't feed her own goldfish), acting like a second parent to your disorganized younger brother, keeping up your grades and top-dog position at school, and trying not to get eaten alive in the school jungle. Worse, those pesky siblings are always in your space, ruining your stuff, messing up your homework, and interrupting your plans when you are called on to babysit them.

You're reliable, conscientious, a list-maker, and a black-and-white thinker. You have a keen sense of right and wrong and believe there is a "right way" to do things. You feel like you always have to be right and perfect, or you'll let the adults in your life down.

Firstborn Traits
1. perfectionist
2. achiever
3. leader
4. can be seen as bossy
5. responsible
6. motivated
7. conscientious
8. controlling
9. cautious
10. reliable

If you're an only child, you feel all the things that a first-born does (minus sibling annoyances), only times 10. After all, you're the sole kid in the family. You feel like *everything* rests on you, so everything you do is magnified. Mom and Dad have only you to look at and focus on. Worse, you find it difficult to identify with your peers. They seem juvenile and silly, since you are used to relating to only adults at home.

Books are your best friends, and you feel most comfortable with alone time. You act mature beyond your years. You were a little adult by age seven or eight. You also love to work independently. You can't stand others dropping the ball. You feel like you have to pick it up by default.

Only Child Traits
1. confident
2. conscientious
3. responsible
4. perfectionist
5. center of attention
6. mature for their age
7. seek approval
8. sensitive
9. leader

What you need most as a firstborn or only child.

- Unconditional love, acceptance, and respect from your teacher.

- To know that your place as part of the classroom community is secure. You are a valued, contributing member.

- The opportunity to share thoughts, feelings, opinions, and research, but not to always be in the spotlight.

- To know you don't need to be perfect. The world won't end if you get a B on a paper or forget your lunch one day.

- To be told that failure is okay. It's a natural part of learning and figuring out what doesn't work, so you can figure out next what can work.

- To know that you don't have to pick up after others in the classroom. If they drop the ball, they are responsible and accountable for their own choices.

- To know that you don't have to do everything. You can pick and choose.

- For others to realize that you don't need their criticism. You're already hard enough on yourself.

- To be allowed some space and quiet to regroup and think more deeply about subjects.

- Time to talk one-on-one with the teacher, because adults were your world before any siblings came along. You're more comfortable with adults than your peers.

If You're a Middleborn

You often wonder, *Would anyone notice if I went missing?*

You feel invisible, squished between Ms. Star and the little pipsqueak who gets attention no matter what he does because he's "cute." When your siblings fight, you keep your mouth shut, lay low, and simply watch the fireworks. If you can, you exit stage left until the fuss is over. You'd rather avoid all conflict entirely. If you have to intervene, you play mediator because you want quiet waters in the house again. You're good at seeing multiple sides of an issue and finding compromises, but that doesn't mean you like to do that.

No one takes time to ask what you think or feel. They couldn't hear you anyway over the noisy baby. Sometimes you feel like an alien in your own family, with hardly any photos of you unless you're lodged between your siblings. That's why friends are so important, and you're loyal.

You walk to the beat of a different drummer. You have no interest in competing with your firstborn sibling. You'd rather go your own way, which often means the opposite direction. If anybody expects you to be like that sibling who preceded you in last year's class, well, they're way off....

Middleborn Traits
1. adaptable
2. independent
3. go-between
4. people-pleaser
5. can be rebellious
6. feels left out
7. peacemaker
8. social

What you need most as a middleborn.

- Unconditional love, acceptance, and respect from your teacher.

- To know that your place as part of the classroom community is secure. You are a valued, contributing member.

- To know that what you think and feel matters and to be asked your thoughts, feelings, and opinions since you're not likely to volunteer them.

- To be allowed opportunities to develop a good core group of friends, since they'll be a key part of your life.

- To know that it's okay to tell the teacher when classmates step out of line and hurt you.

- To know that it's right and healthy to speak up and stand up for yourself.

- To be encouraged to pursue your areas of specific strength.

- To not always have to play peacemaker between your classmates since you always have to with your siblings.

- Time to spend one-on-one with the teacher but not a face-to-face sitdown, since that feels like a confrontation, which you avoid. You like walking and talking or doing an activity together much better.

If You're the Lastborn

You're the little charmer, the fledgling in the nest who gets the most attention because you're always up to something. You're uncomplicated, spontaneous, humorous, and high on people skills. You're the entertainer in your family and at school. You're also the family's sacrificial lamb. When your siblings want something from Mom or Dad, who do they send? You, the one most likely to accomplish the mission without getting killed. Besides, if you catch an earful for asking, your older sister thinks, *It's about time. You deserve it.*

After all, you know exactly how to get her in trouble. You're a natural-born manipulator. One touch, a scream like you've been stabbed, and Mom comes running like a trained dog to rescue her baby. You act incapable so your older brother will do for you what you should do for yourself, like tying your shoes or assembling the contents of your backpack. He does it out of self-protection too. He knows it'll get done faster that way so he can go about his business. Otherwise, Dad will blame him for your work if it isn't done. That's also why that brother still treats you like a baby and doesn't show you any respect.

You're the social, outgoing kid who loves to have fun. You've never met a stranger. You can befriend a rock. Clearly you have skills, yet people don't tend to take you seriously. It's easy to fulfill expectations when people don't have any of you.

Lastborn Traits
1. social
2. charming
3. outgoing
4. uncomplicated
5. manipulative
6. seeks attention
7. self-centered
8. focused on fun

What you need most as a lastborn.

- Unconditional love, acceptance, and respect from your teacher.

- To know that your place as part of the classroom community is secure. You are a valued, contributing member.

- To know that your contributions are not only wanted but needed in the group.

- To learn that life isn't a party 24/7. Sometimes you have to do real work too.

- To learn how to think through situations to the consequences before you act.

- To realize that you don't always have to be the center of attention. Others deserve their time in the limelight too.

- To learn that homework doesn't get done on its own. You have to do it.

- To learn that if you don't follow the rules, accountability follows. You might miss a fun time like recess.

- To learn that cuteness and manipulation can only take you so far. It might work on your siblings a lot of the time, but you won't win friends and neighbors in class with that tactic.

- To be treated with respect so you'll rise to the challenge.

- To be allowed to use your natural entertaining skills—to help others laugh and de-stress—to benefit rather than distract your classmates.

- To have learning be fun, with lots of opportunities for social interaction.

Understand birth order, and you are way ahead of the game of the majority of teachers. Now you know why your students, their parents, and your colleagues act like they do. That knowledge will come in mighty handy at school and in life outside the classroom.

The New ABCs

Take a careful look at the first two items under each birth order's "What you need most" listing. Don't they look familiar?

You're right. They're the same under each category. No matter their birth order, all students need unconditional love, acceptance, and respect from their teacher. They also need to know that their place in the classroom community is secure, and that they are a valued, contributing member. Those two shared items point toward what all your students want most. They want to be **A**ccepted, to **B**elong somewhere, and to be viewed as **C**ompetent in their ability to contribute. Craft your classroom culture to meet the ABC needs, and you'll never go wrong.

Acceptance

Contrary to how it might seem, all students crave your approval and live up to your expectations for them. That's why it's important to set high expectations. Allow students to rise rather than fall to your expectations. Not allowing them to do things on their own is telling them, "You're the dumbest kid I've ever seen," and "I don't think you can do it by yourself, so I have to help." But with an approving nod and a "Go for it! I know you can do it!" attitude, your students will fly high and keep going for a long time on that kind of wind.

Acceptance comes via your words and your actions. Students want to be noticed, to be listened to, to be liked, and to feel special. None of those wants take much time. A smile, a nod, a look, a few words, a note here or there is all it takes to influence a child's life forever. Isn't that worth a few minutes of your precious time?

An Apple a Day

Five Tips to Keep Communication Open

1. View life from behind their eyes.

2. Allow your student time to process.

3. Listen, listen, and listen.

4. Make sure what you're saying and what you're doing matches.

5. Be open 24/7.

Belonging

Every student longs to belong somewhere. What's critical is *where* they choose to belong. Will it be as a member of your classroom community, where it's safe to try and fail? Or out on their own in the quagmire of social media, where one mistake can float around for years and impact their job possibilities someday? Be intentional about offering and ensuring that every child has a unique role in your classroom. Students will never feel secure or like a part of your "family" unless they are able to contribute to the group.

Competence

Want your students to gain psychological muscle to power through any hurdle that comes their way in school or in life? Then empower them by giving them responsibility. When they follow through, say, "Good job. I bet it feels good to finish that project." If they don't complete that task, or they do it poorly, then reality does the teaching. Either way, your students have learned something. In the first scenario, they've learned how good it feels when they have worked hard for something, completed that something, and can call it their own. In the second scenario, they've learned what happens when they don't follow through, or when they don't give that project their best shot. Then they can decide how to do things differently the next go 'round.

When children feel accepted, when they feel like they belong to your classroom, and that you and their classmates see them as competent in the way they contribute, healthy self-worth starts to grow. Relationships flourish. Students feel ready for more complex tasks. As their responsibility increases, so does their confidence in their ability to master challenges of any kind.

What Types of Students Do You Have?

See how many you can identify in your classroom.

The Thrill Seeker

Often loud and charismatic, they enjoy being in the middle of everything. They have great people skills and are good at drawing attention to themselves.

The Wallflower

They feel safe on the fringes, hope to go unnoticed, and fear attention. Criticism seems fatal.

The "It's All About Me"

These students tend to be self-centered and act as if the world revolves around them. They reign supreme among their peers.

The Middle-of-the-Road

Their motto of peace at any price makes them waffle back and forth. As a result they exhibit few leadership skills and often aren't tapped for such roles.

The Anti-Establishment Rebel

They are against anything you say. Everything from their hairstyles, to clothing, to attitudes declares, "I'm not going to be what you want me to be."

The Missionary

These on-task movers and shakers seem too good to be true. They have highly developed value systems and a strong sense of responsibility. They are always "on a mission."

The Aggressor

They can throw negative comments and the occasional punch at other students like nobody's business. They are driven by insecurity but long for love, acceptance, and a secure place among the pack.

How You Can Help

1. Be predictable. Do what you say and say what you'll do.

2. Encourage their strengths and talents. Students need to see themselves as good at something.

3. Be real. Be authentic. Share a time you failed…and lived to tell about it.

4. Provide opportunities for them to make age-appropriate choices and discover the results of those choices. There's nothing like a little reality to file off rough personality edges.

5. Keep everything in perspective. Remember that they are still kids. They will change clothing and hairstyles. They will try on personalities. They will role-play. And they'll need you more than they'll ever admit.

Your Opportunity Awaits

You have an awesome opportunity to assist in molding kids like wet cement in beneficial ways. But you can only do that if you first understand them. Sometimes sidewalks are straight. Other times they zigzag. Artistic ones can be round circles, look like snakes in the grass, or be dotted with handprints or footprints. What do they have in common? They all have borders. You supply the borders, which are the classroom rules, your high expectations, your relationship with your students, and the safe, energetic, learning-conducive community. What happens *within* those borders as students learn, explore, and discover how to achieve their personal bests will vary greatly because those students are individuals with their own gifts.

Some students will follow the path you expect. Other students will surprise you. But each one will be fueled by high expectations. Take Mama Leman, for example. Her final grade in algebra was the same as mine, a 22. Yes, you read that right. That's 22 out of 100. Yet she ended up becoming a nurse and later the hardworking superintendent of a convalescent home for children. No wonder she had the patience and foresight to believe the best of me, despite all that evidence to the contrary. She had seen it fulfilled in her own life.

Regardless of the grade that you teach, students need a personal connection with you to let their guard down and trust that you are truly invested in their success. That means you must get to know each of them as unique individuals with strengths, weaknesses, likes, dislikes, goals, and dreams.

You may be wondering, *How can I possibly squeeze one more thing into my schedule? I hardly have a minute to myself as it is.* We understand. Teachers' days are filled to the brim and overflowing. It might help to consider the strategy of personally investing in students, seeking to understand their views and experiences, and what they need from a different lens. This proactive plan helps to eliminate misbehaviors, lack of engagement and participation, and other future problems that could take a lot more of your time.

How is this possible? If students have a personal connection with you and believe you are invested in them, they are much more likely to do their homework, listen to your directions, do what you ask, and live up to your high expectations.

They will assist in a smooth-running classroom. They'll put out behavioral fires before they get started. If you like and respect a teacher, you're much less likely to pull any shenanigans.

One goal I always set for myself was to make each student in my classroom believe that he or she was my favorite student. That goal helped me keep on track with how I treated my students and what I chose to say or not say. It prompted me to *respond* rather than *react,* and solidified my resolve to always offer encouragement, rather than praise.

> If students have a personal connection with you and believe you are invested in them, they are much more likely to do their homework, listen to your directions, do what you ask, and live up to your high expectations.

Your attitude determines the atmosphere in the room and also how safe students feel. The higher the relational connection, the more students know that, no matter what comes along during the school day, you are their advocate. You won't give up on any student in the class, nor will you compromise on your class as a community. This feeling of "we're all in this together" will go a long way for children who are craving the ABCs.

An Apple a Day

Join students for a "Lunch Bunch" where they eat.

Dos:

1. Ask what they did for fun last weekend.

2. Ask about other hobbies or interests and how they discovered they liked them.

3. Look for common ground in your experiences.

4. Give all who want to share a little slice of talking time.

Don'ts:

1. Talk about upcoming assignments.

2. Talk about schoolwork or classroom tasks at all.

3. Pressure students to talk. This is lunch, not interrogation.

Building Classroom Community

Building a classroom community is vital to your students' learning. As a teacher, it's important that you not only place a high value on that process but are intentional about crafting a safe, encouraging, and academically rigorous space. Students need to be able to question, debate, explain, explore, discover, seek clarification, and learn alongside others in a respectful way. But how exactly do you create such a respectful community of learners?

It all starts with you. How do you greet your students daily? How do you speak to them during class? How do you view them? Your classroom is a reflection of your views and attitudes toward them as learners, so be intentional in the messages you are sending in your room as you set it up. Do you display posters, books, and resources that recognize and celebrate the diversity in your class? Will every child feel like they belong in your room? Have you conveyed your care for them as individuals?

I used to eagerly await my class list so I could start bedazzling students' names on everything in the room. But more importantly, I'd begin to look through my own collection of books to find stories with my students' names in the book or in the title. I used to begin or end the day with one of these books until I had checked off each student in my class. I wanted to show them that I cared by reading a story *just for them.*

Reading to students of any age is a powerful technique for building community. If you are an elementary school teacher, you can gain tremendous mileage through the purposeful reading of books that personally reflect students in your class. If you teach middle school or high school, don't assume picture books are too elementary. Many picture books have subject matter that is a best fit for middle-school students and can be a platform for debate and discussion.

I once had to step into a class to sub for a few minutes while a teacher had to step away. There was no time for her to tell me the lesson plan. What did I do? I grabbed a book off my shelf to read to that sixth-grade class. Since the virtue of humility was the current schoolwide topic, *The Giving Tree* by Shel Silverstein was perfect. Before reading it, I asked the students if any of them had heard this story before. Only a few hands went in the air. I read the book aloud, modeling expression and feeling as I walked around the room. The class was well behaved and listened intently to the story.

After finishing the book, I had students stand and vote with their feet. I divided the room into two sections. One side of the room was "the tree" and the other side was "the boy." I asked students to pause and reflect on which they would rather be, the tree or the boy. I asked them to show their vote by moving to that side of the room.

Immediately students began to move to the two sides of the room. A handful of students stood on the side designated for "the boy," and the rest of the class went to "the tree" side. I asked students from each side to explain why they made their choice. At first there were the typical silly answers. But then the discussion got more serious. Students began sharing.

I looped in the virtue of humility, and we compared and contrasted the characteristics of the boy and tree through this lens. I stood in awe of what was transpiring in that classroom:

sixth-graders were speaking of selfishness and contrasting it with humility. They were reflecting on their own personal lives and pondering if they were more like the tree or like the boy, and talking about the impact that had on their family, friends, and classmates.

> Reading to students of any age is a powerful technique for building community.

A few moments later, the classroom teacher returned, and I thanked the class for allowing me to read this story to them. Later that day I returned to my desk to find a note from one of the sixth-grade girls. She stated in the note that she'd never heard that powerful story before, thanked me for sharing it with her, and said she would be mindful of being less like the boy and more like the tree. I sat quietly, appreciating the note and her self-reflection. Moments like that make me especially thankful for my penchant to gather an arsenal of books in my office.

Books, you see, have always been my main source of building community in the classroom. I began to organize my books by the character traits they taught, jotting down those traits in the front cover of the book. As my library grew, I needed a better organizational system, so I made a Google doc and began categorizing my books by the values that they taught. I have categories for playground issues, stealing, being a good friend, showing kindness, each of the character traits and virtues that my school teaches, and so much more. This table is helpful since I can now easily pull books that I need as different classroom issues surface.

Other books I intentionally read at the beginning of year to serve a specific purpose. Many of these books focus on students' names, accepting others, and being part of a team. I often read the class a story and then have them sign the front cover that I photocopy as a way of showing they are "all in" to the message the book conveys. Each student chooses their favorite color marker and signs their name in their best handwriting.

One of my go-to books to read in the first days of school is *Teammates,* by Peter Golenblock. It beautifully retells the story of Pee Wee Reese, Jackie Robinson, and the Los Angeles Dodgers. The last line of the book is so poignant that I usually tear up reading it. I use the message of the book to develop a sense of community in my class: that we *are* teammates, that all of us are on the *same* team, and that we are *all* going to stick together and support each other this year. It certainly is a book that could be read to any age group as it tackles issues of race, acceptance, prejudice, injustice, and breaking racial barriers.

If you haven't yet started your book collection, why not do so now? It will be a treasure trove to build classroom community. Besides, it gives all of your well-wishing family and friends a sweet little something to do to encourage you in your journey as a teacher. Hint that they gift you a book, new or used, from your list.

> If you haven't yet started your book collection, why not do so now? It will be a treasure trove to build classroom community.

Some of the best overall advice we can give about becoming a great teacher by Friday can be stated in two words: be proactive. We've already explored being proactive in establishing your education foundation on Monday. On Tuesday we discussed proactively managing your classroom and crafting its atmosphere. Today we've already given an example of a great way to build community through a careful selection of books to enhance learning and prompt active engagement. Following are seven other ways you can proactively build a respectful classroom community.

#1: Be proactive at the beginning of the year.

No child of any age likes to walk cold into a new classroom on the first day of school. Meeting teachers can also be scary. Take the edge off those worries by introducing yourself briefly in a snail-mail letter to students and their parents that goes out several weeks before school starts. Address the envelope to the student. Why snail-mail, and why address the envelope to the student? Children of all ages love to get personal mail addressed to them.

Give a warm welcome and tell them something about you that would be interesting to that age of student. Define your classroom as an energetic, safe learning environment where you all work hard and play hard together. State your enthusiasm and high expectations for what you will achieve as a team. Invite the student and his or her parents or guardians to meet you before school begins and tour the classroom. Your school might have an already scheduled Meet the Teacher time window or a Back-to-School Night that accomplishes this purpose. Make sure to handwrite a specific note to each student at the end of the letter such as, "I can't wait to meet you, Julianne! We're going to have a great year together."

By doing these small gestures, you are already setting yourself up as an authoritative teacher for the year. Clearly, you're in charge, and you have high expectations. But you're also showing that you emphasize relationships. And here's the bonus: meeting your students and parents before school gives you a peek into their home life and the way they operate. Some will rush in breathless at the last minute. Others will come early and linger. Some will be comfortable and ask good questions. Others will be a bit nervous and try hard to please you. Still others will try their hand at seeing if you'll let them run the show. That small meeting will tell you a lot and allow you to be proactive in your preparation with each student and family.

An Apple a Day

Before the school year begins, send a letter home to your students and their families.

1. Introduce yourself.

2. Briefly describe your classroom as a vibrant, caring, learning community.

3. Set your expectations that each student will achieve their personal bests.

4. Invite them to meet you and tour your classroom before school begins.

#2: Set time aside for students to share with you.

Once school starts, schedule Lunch Buddy Dates with several students in your class at a time to get to know one another better. Yes, this will take a few of your lunchtimes. But if you make it fun, like setting a picnic on the floor of your classroom, even older students will lean in and engage with you.

This is time well spent that will pay off in huge dividends throughout the school year. It's certainly better than sitting in meetings after school with a student's parents, social worker, principal, or any other school representative as you devise a behavior-change plan. As a seasoned coach once told me about his players, "They don't care how much you know until they know how much you care." It's true of your students and their families too.

I once observed an elementary teacher who would not allow her students to interrupt her time and her lessons while she was teaching. She was firm but fair and had a proactive strategy that totally eliminated behavior problems in the classroom.

When it was time for students to go to recess, she would invite anyone who had something to share with her to stay inside and chat. Students would form a line 20 deep to share that they had a wiggly tooth or that they won their soccer match last night.

> They don't care how much you know until they know how much you care.

That authoritative teacher sat and attentively listened to each student. She looked each one in the eye and thanked them for sharing that tidbit with her. Yes, she had the luxury of not having to be on recess duty, but the learning that took place in her room was second to none. She invested in her students and truly showed concern for their little stories. In return, she had a classroom of students that she easily and beautifully managed because each student knew she loved and cared for them as individuals.

Put on your brainstorming cap. Figure out the best way for you to set time aside in your schedule for students to share with you. This is a proactive win-win.

#3: State your positive expectations and belief in your students.

I didn't intend to double-major in Psychology and Elementary Education at North Park University. It was only through the encouragement of psychology professor Haddon (Don) Klingberg that I did so. Double-majoring meant taking on a heavy load, including summer school. But the classes were enjoyable and came with high support from the professors.

Dr. Klingberg was intelligent, thoughtful, and challenging in his class material. He had high expectations and carried them out in such a positive way that his students worked hard to meet them. His priority was investing in students. He related to us as people first, checking in with us, and encouraging our academic success through building relationships with us. He'd frequent the cafeteria and anywhere else students routinely gathered, attend events, and had an open door policy where students could drop in, ask questions, or chat anytime. He knew our names, learned our stories, and shared his field experiences in a way that always emphasized the human factor. He often checked in on students like me, who were attending school many miles from home.

I'll never forget the day he called on me in class to explain the difference between positive and negative reinforcement. I explained what he had taught us, what I had read about, and added my own personal understanding of the differences. He smiled, told me I was right, and that I explained it well. He said that psychologists in the field still couldn't articulate the difference between the two. That single event, added to his many other encouragements, made me feel like all my hard studying was paying off.

As I entered the workforce in education, Dr. Klingberg's example of excellence, kindness, and relationship-building greatly shaped my own philosophy of education. I realized that it is healthy and good to have high expectations and regularly state your positive expectations to your students. It's also important to offer them sincere encouragement when they are on task and doing their best work. Be their champion and their cheerleader. All children crave attention. If they don't get it for positive things that they are doing, they will dream up some negative ones to make you pay attention to them.

It's also acceptable to let students know when you are disappointed in their behavior from time to time. Regardless of the age you teach, no one likes to know that someone else is disappointed in them. Simply state that you expect more because you believe they can do better. But the authoritative, relational teacher doesn't stop there. He makes himself available to help turn the behavior around. Students need to know that they and you are all on the same team. You're not working *against* each other but rather *for* each other.

Years after I graduated from North Park, my younger sister graduated. It happened to be the year that Dr. Klingberg was going to retire. I was grateful to see him again, to share my personal thanks, and to congratulate him on the lifelong work that influenced so many.

To Ponder...
High achievement always takes place in the framework of high expectations.
CHARLES KETTERING

#4: Get to the root cause of the behavior.

Have you ever voiced your frustration over students calling out? Regardless of the reminders you provide and the class rules that state, "I will raise my hand," some students continue to call out without following your expectations. *Why can't they follow the rules?* you wonder. But let's take a closer look at what contributes to calling out.

First, do you provide adequate time throughout the day for students to turn and talk? Do they have ample opportunities to share their ideas, ask questions, justify their thinking, and be active participants in the classroom? All students need time to interact with their classmates. If you don't provide such interaction, they'll devise their own plans.

Moving student desks around to quiet chattiness isn't a winning play. Take it from a talkative first grader. Evidently he was getting tired of being moved around, so he did something proactive. He wrote a note: "Dear Teacher, if you move me, I will still talk. I will have a new kid to talk to." That teacher got the message loud and clear.

Second, are your expectations realistic? Are you requiring students to sit quietly for long periods of time? In the upper grades, students are capable of this. But that doesn't mean you shouldn't provide time for movement and talk. Middle-schoolers need social interaction since so much of their culture focuses around their social lives. Instead of working against your students' natural tendencies to communicate, try planning lessons that are engaging, interactive, and collaborative. Such lessons place students at the heart of the lesson, as opposed to you, the teacher, standing and delivering your lecture.

> All students need time to interact with their classmates. If you don't provide such interaction, they'll devise their own plans.

Third, have you properly trained your students on raising their hands? Do they know when it's okay to call out and when hands are required? It may be time to reteach what you want students to do until the habit is formed.

Are you aware of the types of questions you're asking? If they are open-ended, they invite students to answer and create chaos. Consider this open-ended question: "Does everyone have a pencil?" Inevitably students, especially in the younger grades, will reply to your question. Now the room resounds with "yes," "no," "I can't find my pencil," and "someone took my pencil" comments. It would be far better to state, "Raise your hand if you need a pencil." A simple tweak in the way you phrase a request can have a big impact.

With any behavior, you need to get to the root cause of why it's happening. Sometimes you can unintentionally and unknowingly be a part of the problem. If you discover that's the case, then good for you. Now that you know why, you'll be able to brainstorm how to creatively resolve that behavior and then craft a roadmap to effect change. That's what this book is all about—becoming a great teacher by Friday—and you've uncovered another way to get there.

#5: Consider the ratio of interactions.

When I was growing up, I remember sometimes saying something unkind or rude to my siblings. Inevitably, my mom would then make me say three nice things to try to soothe the wound. Well, she was right to do so, and then some.

Did you know that for every negative interaction you have with a student, you need *five* positive ones to offset the impact of the negative one?[11] Also, that negative interaction tends to only be seconds long, the research says. It may be a sharp word, a disappointing comment, or calling out the student in front of the class for misbehavior.

Let's be honest. Some students in your class are easier to like than others. Students instinctively know if you like them or don't like them. So do their peers. Unfortunately, there are students sitting in classrooms who are known as the kid the teacher doesn't like or always picks on.

LEMANISM #10

Teach in such a way
that every student believes
he or she is your favorite.

As with all the strategies in this book, the change has to begin with you. That's why, when you do need to hold a student responsible and accountable, you never do it publically. You pull aside that student and talk to them *privately*. You choose your words wisely. You calmly address the behavior that needs to change and let reality be the teacher. You never accuse, nag, or belittle that student as a person. You retain and grow your relationship with that student by saying things like, "I don't see you that way," "I could be wrong but…," "I believe in you," and "I'm proud of you for doing the right thing now when it is hard to do so."

An Apple a Day

Write #Notes to intentionally encourage your students before a big test. Place the notes on their desks during a break so they return to the surprise.

I'm not telling you it's going to be easy, but it is going to be worth it. Do your best!
Love, Your Teacher #growthmindset

I know this is the first time you are taking this test. Use all the tools and grow your brain!
Love, Your Teacher #growthmindset

#6: Stick to the routines.

A teacher friend once told me a great story about the beginning of the school year. It was nearing the lunch hour. As the class was getting ready for lunch, little Mateo started packing up all his things and put on his backpack. The teacher asked where he was going.

"Home," Mateo said.

The teacher kindly told him he was actually staying for the whole day, having lunch at school, and then he'd be going home later in the day with the big kids.

Mateo frowned. "Who in the world signed me up for this?"

The beginning of the school year can prove to be challenging, regardless of the grade you teach. There are new routines, procedures, and expectations to establish as you meet your new group of students. The start of kindergarten brings additional stressors for parents and teachers alike. Parents are sending their little ones to school for the first time, and students are away from their parents for longer hours as well. Students who were in day-care or a Pre-K program may be more accustomed to spending the day in school. Nonetheless, we can guarantee there will be struggles.

In this time of transition, long days, tiredness, and uncertainty, it's critical to stick to your game plan. Routine gives students a warm sense of security. That's why it's so important to establish and maintain habits you want to maintain all year long. Do so, and the rest of the year will be smooth.

It takes a tremendous amount of effort, intentionality, purpose, direction, and clarity to create a high-functioning classroom on the front end. But the benefits for individual students and the entire classroom community are extraordinary...not to mention the joy you experience that comes with seeing life change.

> Routine gives students a warm sense of security.

#7: To get respect, you have to give respect.

Years ago, I had accepted a new teaching position at a small school and was excited about the opportunity. As a kind gesture, the principal invited me to their annual outdoor concert so I could get a feel for the school. I was happy to attend, since many students and their families would likely be there. During that time, multiple families approached me, warmly introduced themselves, and welcomed me.

However, the longer I lingered, the more I started to realize a theme. Family after family had mentioned to me that I did not want a particular boy in my class next year. I was perplexed and stunned at the multiple comments about this boy whom I had never met. I also didn't imagine that I would have any say in who was in my class and who was not. So, I tucked the name away in my mind and waited until the fall for my class list.

Sure enough, the boy I had been adamantly warned about was right there on my class list. Elijah. I'd be lying if I said I wasn't a bit nervous. But, more than that, my determination kicked in to get to know that little guy and figure him out. I'd grown up in a family that always treated people with respect and stuck up for any underdog.

It didn't take long for Elijah to make himself known to me. You've heard the expression "a bull in a China shop"? Well, that was Elijah. He was big for his age and had an aggressive edge. I quickly learned that everyone in school was afraid of him, since his reputation had preceded him.

On the first day of school, a girl came up to me at recess and said very matter-of-factly, "Nobody likes Elijah."

I had barely gotten to know him as it was only the first day, but I had a feeling in my gut that this would be a defining moment. I looked her straight in the eye and told her I didn't like her saying that about her classmate and that I liked him.

She appeared stunned. She regarded me as if I were incredibly naïve to all the pranks Elijah had pulled off. She told me about the time he hid behind a wall and punched whoever walked by in the arm.

I told her honestly I was unaware of that but promised her that Elijah would be different this year. She raised a dubious eyebrow.

That exchange made me more determined to turn the train around. I quickly got to know Elijah's siblings who were also in the school and invited his parents in to meet with me and share about his likes and dislikes. I worked hard at my relationship with him by keying in on his interests. I also diffused any negative comments that I heard about him. After all, he was now one of *my* kids. I didn't like anyone speaking negatively about *any* of my kids.

I knew I had to change the narrative about Elijah among the students, other teachers, administrators, and parents alike. No one had forged that path before. They simply continued to spin negative talk about him. All that did was tell Elijah what others expected of him, and he was simply living up to those negative expectations.

As the year went on, the chatter surrounding Elijah slowly changed. I became his advocate. None of his classmates or any other students in the school messed with him. He stopped messing with other kids. It was truly a 180-degree change in that second-grader's life.

Numerous families, administrators, and other teachers would inquire from time to time about what I had done to make Elijah change his attitude and behavior at school. I would smile and say, "I didn't make him change his attitude and behavior. He did that all on his own. When you expect the worst, you'll likely get the worst. But when you expect the best, you'll also likely get the best." The answer was quite simple, actually. I loved him, and I believed in him.

An important part of building a positive classroom community is advocating for your class and its success at all costs. There might be an "Elijah" in your class right now. Why not be willing to be the instrument of change for that student? The change you see will likely leave an indelible imprint on his heart and on your own.

An Apple a Day

7 Tips to Building Classroom Community

1. Be proactive at the beginning of the year.
2. Set time aside for students to share with you.

3. State your positive expectations and belief in your students.

4. Get to the root cause of the behavior.

5. Consider the ratio of interactions.

6. Stick to the routines.

7. To get respect, you have to give respect.

The Rest of Isla's Story

Remember Isla and the red heart that brought her comfort? Well, all *was* well in her world at school…until that stone heart went missing. We were working away on our math lesson when I heard a loud *clank, clank, clank*. Something had dropped and skipped across that smooth cement floor.

I knew immediately it had to be Isla's heart. My own heart sank. *Oh, no. We just got over that hurdle. Will we have to start all over again? Will she cry?*

Isla looked at me with tears in her eyes. I knew I had to respond and not react, as stressful as this moment was. My class was well aware of her struggle to transition to kindergarten and that she missed her mom. So, I took advantage of our growing kindergarten community and enlisted the help of every single classmate.

"Okay, class," I said, "Isla lost her heart rock, and we can't seem to find it. It has to be here somewhere. When I say 'Go!' I want you to look for that heart. Ready, set, go!"

Off the students went, searching all around the room for that heart. A red-headed boy named Grayson suddenly popped up from behind the area where the backpacks were hung. "I found it!" he happily announced.

Isla was overjoyed. The class cheered as Grayson returned it to her, and she hugged it to her heart. At that moment, I was proud of myself. *(It's okay, you can be proud of yourself when you choose to do the right thing.)* It had been such a long emotional road to get Isla settled in kindergarten. I was proud that I didn't get mad or reprimand her for dropping that heart rock and interrupting the math lesson. Instead my training and determination to know, understand, and respect each child's uniqueness kicked in.

I found a better way. I chose to rally the class as a group to help her solve the problem in a way that honored her. Not only that, her classmates were high-fiving each other and grinning because they'd been able to be a part of the solution. Plus, who doesn't want a surprise break in the middle of math class? It was a win-win for Isla, for the other students, and for my relationship with all the students.

Fast forward to the end of that school year. Students began to sweetly bring me thank-you notes, coffee mugs, and other goodies. Isla came up shyly and handed me a bag. I was eager to look inside. Over the course of that year, I had grown to love that dear girl, along with her sensitivity and passion for the little things of life.

I reached into the bag. Inside was a yellow polished stone heart that resembled the red stone heart she'd held at the beginning of the school year. I was touched at the meaningful, priceless gift. To this day, it sits on my desk as a reminder to always carefully shepherd each little heart in my care.

Winning Play #4
Get Real with Relational Discipline

*The Leman Way allows real-life consequences
to be the teacher.*

What would you do if your student didn't bring his gym clothes?
Or wore clothes that broke the school rules? For the first week of
sixth grade, Jackson sat on the sidelines of PE because he didn't
bring his gym clothes. Lucas, an eighth grader, routed school
rules about no logos or faces on clothing when he wore the same
rapper long-sleeved T-shirt. Lin, a seventh grader, decided to
invent her own definition of "appropriate attire."

What did all three of these middle-schoolers share in
common? A desire to do things differently from the norm and
to not follow the school's rules. The first couple of days, their
teachers simply dismissed the infractions as part of an adjust-
ment period.

But by day three, they felt they had to talk *to* the students
and state that they needed to follow the rules. So, they talked *at*
the students privately and laid down the law. The students kept
doing what they were doing. They didn't adjust.

The second week all three teachers decided to do something completely different. The students were accompanied to the Lost & Found to find new attire. One private look in the mirror of the locker rooms dressed in that clothing was enough to send each teen a message: "If you don't bring your own clothes that adhere to the school rules, then you won't like the ones you'll have to wear as a result."

The teachers didn't embarrass the students. They were allowed to return to the classrooms in their own clothing. The next day, all three students arrived with the appropriate attire. The ball of responsibility had been put squarely in their court for not adhering to school policy. They were given a wake-up call of what tomorrow could look like in front of their peers if they did not follow the rules.

Problem solved, right? But there's a big problem with the *method* of discipline those teachers chose to use. The students had no relationship with those teachers. The teachers didn't go out of their way to get to know them. The teachers merely talked *to* or *at* those students, rather than *with* them. They merely looked at the *what* of the misbehavior, decided *how* the issues could be resolved, but didn't address the root of the behavior— *why* the behavior was occurring in the first place.

With no relationship, the students didn't care what their teachers thought. They didn't care about the school's rules. They only cared what the consequences of wearing Lost & Found clothes would look like in front of their peers. No middle-schooler likes to be embarrassed. That next day, the students may have adhered to the rules, but rebellion brewed under the surface about what they had been made to do.

To Ponder...

Educating the mind without educating the heart
is no education at all.

ARISTOTLE

Do you want your students to achieve their personal best in your classroom? Do you love your students? If so, you will discipline them. The best way for students to learn how to be responsible is to be given age-appropriate choices. The best way for students to learn about accountability is to live the consequences of their choices, both positive and negative.

This chapter will address how to discipline a different, better, and proactive way. It's a way that works *every single time.* We'll uncover why students misbehave and reveal how behavior progresses if left unchecked. We'll explore the 7 Principles of Relational Discipline. And, finally, we'll tie together how what you say and do makes all the difference in the choices that your students will make.

The Goals of Misbehavior

Did you know that all behavior is *purposive?* Bet you haven't used that word much today. What it means is simply this: all behavior serves a purpose. Remove that purpose, and there is no need for the behavior.

You can address the behavior by talking *to* or *at* students all day long, keep them after school in detention, and that behavior still won't turn around. But if you talk *with* students and begin to understand *why* they are behaving a certain way, you can get to the root of the issue and address the underlying need.

LEMANISM #11

All behavior is purposive.
It serves a purpose.
Remove that purpose,
and there's no longer
a need for that behavior.

Think about the three middle-schoolers at the start of this chapter. Imagine that you are having a conversation with each of those students. As you talk, you discover the following information. Would it change your perspective of their behavior?

Jackson hasn't been bringing gym clothes because he thinks he's terribly uncoordinated. He's deeply afraid his classmates will laugh at him if he can't shoot hoops or dribble a basketball. He's stalling to get through the weeks the PE teacher has assigned to teach that sport.

Lucas overly wears the rapper shirt because it's now his favorite. He recently discovered his love for rap music. He's been secretly writing his own rap lyrics and rapping in his bedroom when no one is at home. From the quick view he's shown you, the lyrics are all about figuring life out. They're actually pretty good. They're meaningful, positive, and sometimes funny.

Lin lives under the weight of authoritarian parents who dictate everything about her life, including what she can wear to school. Her parents bought clothes they deemed appropriate without her input. She hates the style they picked but doesn't dare to tell them because she doesn't want to disappoint them. It's no wonder she wears a long coat in 80-degree weather and flees to the restroom before school to change into clothing a friend brings for her. Wearing her parent-chosen clothing would be the end of her social life.

Wow, doesn't knowing those facts about the students and understanding *why* they are behaving that way make all the difference? That's why we say if you eliminate the *need* for the behavior, there is no need for the behavior to continue.

In Jackson's case, that means you as the gym teacher, now aware, change up your class curriculum. You create small-group stations where students can choose which activities they'd like to try. Jackson surprises you and himself by emerging as a killer badminton player. Seeing a smile on the face that previously resembled a stone monument is worth the work of reconfiguring your lesson plans. In fact, all the students love the new approach and are much more willing to try a variety of sports. You're a lifelong learner, so you enjoy finetuning your craft.

And that behavior that bothered you? There's no problem with Jackson remembering his gym clothes anymore. What worked for one student ended up being a win-win for you and the entire class because you took the time to understand that student and why he was behaving that way.

Stages of Misbehavior[12]

All kids are attention getters. They are very perceptive even at an early age. They size up the social atmosphere around them and figure out how to work the system. They're also created to crave connection and attention. Some will do it by getting good grades, pleasing the adults in their lives, or being helpful around the classroom. Others will get it by driving you crazy with their antics so that you have to pay attention. This is *Stage 1: Attention.* In this stage a student believes, *I only count when I am being noticed or served.*

Children who start off as attention getters and don't receive it in a positive way will then focus on getting it in a negative way. They'll move to *Stage 2: Power.*[13] To them, whether the attention is negative or positive, it's still attention, and they realize they're forcing you to give it to them. In this stage a student believes, *I only count when you do what I want or I can do what I want.*

If children still don't get attention, they move to *Stage 3: Revenge.* In this stage, they still want attention but are solely focused on getting it in a negative way. After all, trying to get any attention for doing something good has utterly failed. Therefore, a student believes, *I only count when I can hurt others as I have been hurt by life.* These children are also tragically the ones you see headlined in news as the perpetrators of mass shootings and other incidents.

In the final stage, *Stage 4: Display of Inadequacy or Assumed Disability,* a student simply gives up and retreats from life. These are the kids who are so discouraged that they don't show interest in anything. They turn the fact that they've received no attention inward, instead of outward. They believe, *I'm no good. I can't do anything right, so I won't try to do anything at all.*

Through all these stages, behavior serves a purpose. The root cause of it is a lack of positive attention. Do you see why paying attention to your students is one of the most important aspects of your job as teacher?

The good news is that 99 percent of students who crave attention will remain in *Stage 1: Attention* or *Stage 2: Power.* How can you tell the difference between an attention-seeking student or a power-driven student? It's actually pretty easy.

Does the behavior *annoy* you? If so, he's an attention seeker.

Does the behavior *provoke* you? If so, he's power-driven.

An Apple a Day

The 4 Stages of Misbehavior

Stage 1, Attention: *I only count when I am being noticed or served.*

Stage 2, Power: *I only count when you do what I want or I can do what I want.*

Stage 3, Revenge: *I only count when I can hurt others as I have been hurt by life.*

Stage 4, Display of Inadequacy or Assumed Disability: *I'm no good. I can't do anything right, so I won't try to do anything at all.*

The Leman Way

The goal of relational discipline is to create responsible, accountable students. But to do that, you have to know each one of your students. You have to have a respectful, positive relationship. What works for one student may not work for another.

Relational discipline is based on *actions,* not words. It steers a course between the authoritarian ("My way or the hallway, I'm the one in control") and permissive ("Can't we all just get along? I love you, you know") styles. It is authoritative. It gives students choices so they can learn responsibility but also holds them accountable for the consequences of their choices.

Here's an example. A first-grader forgets her backpack for the second day in a row. Sometimes children are forgetful. Sometimes *you* are forgetful too. On that first day, any proactive teacher who has a student's best interests in mind would have a cupboard of needed items for such moments and would do well to offer that transitioning child grace. After all, when you forget, you appreciate others giving you grace too.

What happens that second day is critical in your relationship and for that child's developing responsibility and accountability. Here is what the different teacher styles would be likely to say and do.

> *Authoritarian teacher:* "This is the second day you forgot your backpack. I told you yesterday that you needed to bring it. You'll miss morning *and* afternoon recess today. Maybe that will help you remember to bring it tomorrow."

> *Permissive teacher:* "Oh, honey, you forgot it again? Well, maybe I can talk to your mom and she can get it packed for you in the car tomorrow. Does that sound good to you?"

Authoritative teacher: Does not say a thing. Instead she waits until it's time for art, which she knows that little first-grader particularly likes. "Okay, class, pull out your crayons and the butter tub I asked you to bring," she says. That student has crayons in her desk but no butter tub. The authoritative teacher doesn't rescue the student and provide a butter tub. The student simply is not able to do the same art project as the other students. All she can do is use her crayons to color on a white piece of paper.

Imagine *you* are that student. Which teaching style is most likely to prompt you to remember that backpack? Relational discipline embraces freedom for the child to choose and accountability for the consequences. The classroom is where students study the lifelong curriculum of decision-making. Sometimes they will choose wisely. Other times they will choose poorly and suffer real-world consequences.

What Discipline Should Not Be

We discussed earlier the differences between punishment and discipline. In short, punishment teaches nothing and plants the concept of a "mean teacher" in your student's mind. Critique a firstborn or only child, and you've doubly reinforced all the perfectionistic pressure he already puts on himself: *Nothing I do is good enough. I'm not good enough. I'll never be good enough.* Call out a middleborn, and that student will retreat further into her turtle shell and shut you out of her social circle completely. Punish a lastborn, and you'll deflate her happy-go-lucky spirit and her desire to come to school at all since it's no fun.

> The classroom is where students study the lifelong curriculum of decision-making.

131

Discipline Is NOT...

- permissive giving in.

- authoritarian declarations.

- reactionary punishment.

- names on the board for misbehavior.

- power struggles between teacher and student.

- ostracizing students in public.

- sending students outside the room to be dealt with.

What Discipline Should Be

Do you really love the students in your class? If so, you will discipline them. But when you do so, you must discipline with dignity, showing them respect. What does that look like?

First, you do it privately. You remind them of a school or classroom rule but never in front of their peers. Discretion is critical. If you can't pull the child aside, wait until later.

Second, if it happens during all-group time, try proximity. Sometimes moving in closer to the off-task student's desk as you walk around the room and pausing slightly will halt the behavior. Other times you might want to catch her attention and signal that you see her and are aware of her behavior.

Third, you always use your students' names in a *positive* way. Never use a student's name in connection with a negative request: "Sofia, eyes up front. You're not paying attention." Remember the power of positive expectations. Expect the best, and you'll likely get the best. Point out off-task behavior in a negative way, and you reinforce that negative behavior.

Fourth, always take note of behavioral issues with specific students and document them. If that behavior continues, you have specific instances where you can discuss the pattern with the child and their parent.

And fifth, remember that your voice is a tool. It can be used for a positive, beneficial purpose to uplift a student or as a negative technique to put down a student. Positive tone encourages development of the whole child. A negative tone will prompt the student to block out your voice entirely.

Discipline Should Be...

- authoritative.

- relational.

- private.

- respectful.

- address the root of the issue.

- encouraging.

The 7 Principles of Relational Discipline

To practice the Leman Way of relational discipline, focus on the following seven principles.

#1: Establish a healthy authority over your students.

You are the authoritative teacher that your students need. Relational discipline starts and ends with you. That's why you should never give that authority away to anyone else, whether another teacher, parent, or administrator. It is to your own and your students' benefit to keep the ball in your court as long as possible. That means personally handling any situation that comes up and not sending that off-task student to detention or the principal's office unless it's the absolute last option.

Most of all, never engage in a power struggle in front of your class with your student. You will always lose that battle. You have way more to lose than the child does. Don't believe us? Think for a minute about the parent whose child throws a fit in the grocery store. Who is the more embarrassed one who usually gives in to the child's manipulation? The same is true with teachers whose students act up in the hallway.

Believe me, your students know who's in charge. If it's not you, it's them. If you aren't consistent, if you don't have clear procedures, and if you aren't prepared for the lesson, they will take over that control. If students don't feel personally connected to you, they may acquiesce to what you ask them to do, but they won't like it. Rebellion will brew under the surface.

> Believe me, your students know who's in charge. If it's not you, it's them.

Using discipline without a relationship might school the mind, but it does not school the heart. You can set all the rules you want for how students *should* behave, but there will be no real behavioral change.

#2: Cultivate your classroom culture.

In Arizona we have an amazing plant called the *saguaro*. It's the largest type of cactus in the United States with a long life span. With care, at 70 years old, it can be around six feet tall. Its first branch doesn't appear until it's at least 75 years old, and it's not considered an adult until it's about 125 years old.[14] It can tolerate drought and significant storms. But ignore any root rot, and that mighty saguaro can topple quickly.

It's the same in your classroom. A positive learning culture must be carefully cultivated and watched over. The tone of your classroom, as we've discussed, is critical to establishing a conducive-to-learning environment. Respect starts with you and spreads from there. Do you want a classroom that is positive and encouraging? Where classmates have a can-do spirit and work together? Then you must intentionally create that relational atmosphere.

Nothing destroys the root of such an atmosphere faster than reacting instead of responding to student misbehavior. Reacting is easy. Simply open your mouth and blurt out whatever is on your mind without thinking of the consequences. Responding is harder. It requires discipline and strategy about how to handle specific situations before they come up. It entails reining in natural human emotions and considering consequences before you speak and act. It means choosing not to fuel your students' flare-ups.

An Apple a Day

Conversation Starters

- I could be wrong…

- I might be out in left field on this…

- I don't have all the facts yet, but let's talk…

- I'd like to hear what you think/your opinion on this…

At the same time, you have to pay attention to core beliefs that could topple the classroom culture you're building. Do students know that they are not the center of the universe? That others matter? That life is not all about them?

Sometimes students need a wake-up call. They need to hear some private perspective from the teacher they respect. "When you did that, your classmates might have interpreted that as you saying, 'I'm the only important one here. Life is all about me.'" Whoa.

It's never too early to learn that life is not all about you. Others matter. They deserve a voice and a place on center stage sometimes too. The culture in your classroom is defined by the lowest accepted behavior.

#3: Win your students' cooperation.

How do you intentionally seek to win your students' cooperation? And what might that look like? Take Lucas, the rap-loving middle-schooler. If you're his authoritative teacher, here's how you might handle the issue of his rule-routing shirt.

> The culture in your classroom is defined by the lowest accepted behavior.

You do some quick research on the rapper featured on the shirt. Then you pull Lucas aside privately after class. He gets that *uh-oh, I'm in trouble* look.

You say, "I've noticed your shirt. That rapper has some pretty good songs. In fact, (you share a few lyrics from one song that you found interesting). If you ever want to talk more about him or rapping, I'd love to."

Lucas stands there open-mouthed. He doesn't say a word. After school, though, he pauses awkwardly in front of you. "Uh, could we talk more about rapping?"

Now that the conversation is *his idea,* information pours out. He shyly shows you some lyrics he's written. They're actually quite good and reveal where his head is at in trying to figure out the world.

LEMANISM #12

The power of positive expectations
changes your conversations.

You say, "You've certainly been working hard on these. I can tell they mean a great deal to you, and the rapper we've talked about inspired you with his style. If you'd ever like to share one with the class, let me know. I think your classmates would especially benefit by hearing your rap about working hard to fit in. I think everybody feels that way sometimes."

His eyes widen. "Thanks, Mrs. G!"

"You're welcome. Oh, and Lucas?" Now you have his full attention because you've shown interest in his hobby. "I know how much that rapper shirt means to you," you say calmly. "But school rules are no logos or faces on shirts. I think your interest in rap can speak for itself, without the shirt, and bring a meaningful flair to class when or if you decide to share it."

He gets the message. Sure enough, there's no rapper shirt in your class the next day. You notice him scribbling notes during brain-break time. You smile. You might have a fun rapping session to share soon with the whole class.

Students need and deserve to be treated with love, care, and respect. If you confront a student in front of his peers, especially in middle school or high school, you will lose your relationship with that student. You will show yourself as untrustworthy. But if you come alongside that student, retain his dignity, and show him respect, he'll not only help you problem-solve the issue, he may fix the problem himself. Sometimes he only needs you to assume the sideline position of coach.

It's always a win-win when you win your students' cooperation.

An Apple a Day

On the first day of school, ask students to fill out a "Favorite Things" worksheet.

It will serve as a private introduction to each child's mind and heart and give you ideas of how to grow your relationship.

#4: Let reality be the teacher.

True or False? The only way a young person learns responsibility is by facing the consequences for his or her actions.

True.

All actions have consequences that can teach lasting lessons, if the student is not rescued. Some consequences will be positive, and some will be negative. Experiencing both is necessary for the development of the whole child.

Letting the reality of the situation be the teacher is a simple process where you allow the child's actions to naturally dictate the consequences. After all, isn't that what happens in real life?

If you don't set your alarm, you're late, and you have to explain why you're late. If you're disorganized and forget your paperwork, you have to redo it during a time that otherwise would be a brain break. If you forget to bring your lunch, you may get a little hungry. If you engage in a war of words, you have to apologize and make amends.

Are those real-life situations uncomfortable? Of course. But, as I always say, "A healthy child is not always a happy child." The same goes for adults.

If you don't allow students to experience the consequences of their choices, you short-circuit the learning process. What students experience for themselves they're not likely to forget.

To Ponder...

No grit, no pearl.

UNKNOWN

138

#5: Let your actions match your words.

Consistency is critical. You must do what you say you'll do.

If you say, "I'll let you go this time, but don't let it happen again," which phrase do you think speaks louder to a student? The words *don't let it happen again* or the action of letting the child off the hook?

What about "I guess you didn't hear my directions the first time, so I'll tell you again"? Which phrase speaks louder?

We could give more examples, but they would all have the same result: The action wins every time. If you want students to accept responsibility for their actions, you cannot let them off the hook. Don't accept excuses, because excuses only make the weak weaker. Always follow through on what you say you'll do.

#6: Focus on the 3 Rs, not rules.

Is your classroom rule-oriented or relationship-oriented? Take a look at the phrase "relational discipline." Did you notice that the word *relational* comes before the word *discipline?* There's a reason for that. Education is not about the rules. It's about having the right relationships. Without first having a relationship, rules mean nothing to a student. In fact, having to adhere to them prompts rebellion.

> Always follow through on what you say you'll do.

We've stated before that every child lives up to the expectations you have for him. Do you provide high expectations and expect the best to get the best? Do you also provide high support for individual students? A proactive, positive-approach partnership with students is the key to relational discipline. And the same type of partnership is paramount to communicating with the home, the subject of the next chapter.

An Apple a Day

Draw a horizontal line on a piece of paper. Label the left side *Rules* and the right side *Relationships*. Place an X where you'd place yourself on the spectrum right now.

How might you be able to better balance the necessity for rules with also deeply valuing the pursuit of relationships?

Remember Lin, the student with the inventive clothing? Here's what you, an authoritative teacher, might do to address that issue. You pull her aside privately for a friendly conversation after school. You approach her gently since you understand birth order and know that she is an only child and greatly feels the weight of representing her family.

"I notice you have a unique outfit on each day," you say. "Clothes must be really important to you."

Her eyes light up. She explains how much she loves fashion and mix-and-matching.

"I couldn't help but notice also that you wear a long coat every morning to school," you say. "If there's anything you want to share with me, I'd appreciate hearing it."

Tears brim. Her frustration and stress pours out. She tells you about her parents buying all her clothes without her input and about the pressure she feels to please them and be perfect. She ends by saying softly, "I wish my parents knew how I felt."

"I understand," you say. "That must really hurt. I can see why you wear a coat and why you change into a friend's clothes every day. I bet you've already brainstormed ways to try to talk to your parents."

"Yeah," she says. Then suddenly she lands on the solution herself. "I'm going to write them a letter."

Two days later Lin races in and twirls to show you her new outfit. Better yet, her mom accompanied her to the thrift store of her choice and let her choose.

At the upcoming parent-teacher conference, both parents arrive looking a bit nervous and embarrassed. Their actions are quite different from the commanding personas they had during your first meeting at Back-to-School Night. They thank you for starting the process of change in their home.

"I had no idea how much pressure Lin felt because of us," the father says.

To Ponder...

Rules without relationships lead to rebellion.

JOSH MCDOWELL

Both parents grew up in homes where their parents called all the shots. They simply followed that parenting style, they confess. Lin's letter shocked them and opened their eyes.

"We love our daughter," the mom says with great emotion, "but now she knows it because we are doing things differently."

It's true that a teacher can change not only one student's life but the trajectory of a whole family. Lin turned into a fashionista on a budget, and her new fashion adhered to the school rules. Behavior solved. As a bonus, Lin became a smiling, confident student, barely recognizable from the rebel with an attitude who walked into your classroom on day one.[15]

Disciplinary interactions shouldn't be single transactions. They should be *transformational*. Transformations like Lin's occur when a teacher keeps in mind the ABCs, that relationships must come before rules, and that everything that happens in the classroom is part of growing the whole student as a learner.

#7: Model the virtues you want to see.

Want your students to be honest? Model honesty. Want your

students to be positive? The buck stops with you. Want your students to be kind? Then be kind. Want your students to pursue excellence? Then do the same in your work. Every classroom should strive for and be known for excellence. But your classroom should never strive for or be known for trying to hit the high bar of perfection. There's no such thing in real life. Attempting to be perfect simply sets students up for a nasty fall and a harsh landing.

That's why I always tell teachers to flaunt their imperfections. Tell your students about times you didn't hit the high bar you shot for. Amazingly, life as you knew it didn't end that day. Though it was rough for a while, things turned out all right. When you give your students permission to fail, they can relax and let new information in. That includes seeing situations from differing perspectives.

LEMANISM #13
Flaunt your imperfections.

Above all, don't forget to purposefully and intentionally feed the 7 Essential Vitamins to your students every day in generous helpings. Your students need them far more than you'll know. For a quick reminder, here they are:

- Vitamin A = Accountability + Attitude

- Vitamin B = Behavioral Expectation

- Vitamin C = Caring + Cooperation

- Vitamin D = Discipline

- Vitamin E = Encouragement

- Vitamin L = Laughter

- Vitamin N = No

An Apple a Day

The next time you grade a paper, don't write "-8" on the paper. Write "+92."

Positivity will win every time in spurring a student onward and upward.

Taking the Long-Term Perspective

Artist Claude Monet is well known for his impressionist paintings of the natural world. But not everyone knows those paintings were based on a first-hand view of his gardens in Giverny, France, now visited by adoring tourists with an eye for masterpieces of beauty. Those gardens did not grow overnight. They were purposefully cultivated over years and years.

Sometimes gardeners simply needed to use trimming shears to shape off-task plants. Other times they had to apply the hedge trimmer since more thorough work was needed. The result of such intentional work not only inspired Monet to paint his classics but continues to inspire millions with his legacy.

As you cultivate the young, tender plants in your classroom, sometimes they'll need a shearing here and there. Other times they might require the hedge trimmer of a partnership between teacher, parent, and student to turn a behavior around. Unlike Monet's garden of a lifetime, you only have one school year. If you use relational discipline, you can inspire not only one child but influence the lives of all those he relates with down the road.

Now that's a masterpiece well worth any work it takes to get there, wouldn't you say?

Friday

Winning Play #5
Master the 5 Ps of Home Partnership

Interactions should be purposeful, persistent, positive,
professional, and proactive.

"Over the last 180 days you've spent with your child, have you ever had to correct or redirect your child?" I asked a group of parents to kick off Back-to-School Night.

As you might imagine, many parents responded with laughter. There were some grins, a lot of head shaking, a mix of contemplative expressions, and a few winces. Of course, the honest answer was "yes," because kids, like their parents, are human beings.

I always looked forward to Back-to-School Night as the beginning of our face-to-face relationship. I proactively set the stage each year by sending a welcome letter home to the student and his family. But Back-to-School Night brought the players directly onto that stage to meet and interact.

I also enjoyed welcoming the parents of my students into my classroom and greeting them individually. I would then explain my expectations to the group, allow them to get to know a little about me, and learn something about them as well. It was valuable time spent in launching the concept of a classroom community that welcomed parent volunteers and partnership between the school and the home.

Why did I ask that opening question that seems, well, a little silly and obvious? Because I wanted to subtly point out that no child is perfect. Over the next 180 days together, as part of a community of learners, their child may need some redirection or a private conversation with a teacher. The parents themselves might need to be in a conference with the teacher.

LEMANISM #14

No child is—or should be—
the center of the universe.

When that happened, I didn't want it to feel like a mountain that they should dread or worry about. Rather it would be like a slight bump in the road where we could stop together, look at the signposts, and figure out the best ways to adjust and journey on. Asking that question set the platform for our relationship for the year.

Next I informed them that I was looking forward to getting to know each of their children as individuals with differing personalities and gifts. I had high expectations for my students academically and behaviorally. I believed every student could achieve their personal best in both areas and would this year. I also explained that I believed teachers and parents are partners in the education of children, so I would inform and include them in that process. By stating those expectations and beliefs up front, I trusted it would reduce any concerns or confusion over what was happening in the classroom.

"By the way," I added with a smile, "if I contact you, don't assume that it's because your child is in trouble. I might be letting you know about something wonderful your child has done or a beneficial character trait I've discovered about him or her. That's what makes school so exciting. It's a learning experience for all of us, and we're doing it together as a community. I look forward to learning from you too. If at any time you have questions or concerns, feel free to contact me directly." Then I supplied easy methods of texting, phone calls, email, or face-to-face appointments.

After our session, I would know that Back-to-School Night had done its job if the parents who looked anxious upon entering the classroom exited it smiling. You see, every parent wants their child to be well-liked by the teacher. They also want their child to succeed (some, granted, want their child to be at the top of the heap). Some of those parents had school success under their own belts. Others had difficult experiences with learning, the peer group, teachers, or other adults when they were in school. Sessions like that assisted me in spreading the word that I would be their child's advocate and the parents' partner, rather than the feared judge, jury, and executioner toward them or their child.

The 5 Ps

If you want to partner successfully with the home, major on the 3 Rs and use the 5 Ps. They're easy to remember and to implement. Not only will they help you start out the year right, they'll keep you and your class moving on smoothly the rest of the year when bumps arise in the road.

#1: Be purposeful.

Education isn't just a day job. It's about setting an atmosphere where students are actively engaged in their own learning, and parents are informed, supportive partners. It's about relational discipline that lets reality do the teaching and preserves your relationship with student and parent. It's about having high expectations of your students and modeling those same expectations. It's about living out the virtues and displaying the essential vitamins. It's about carefully thinking of consequences before you act so you respond rather than react to situations.

It's about investing in your students and working to understand them so you can advocate effectively for them. It's about strategizing how to provide a classroom that gives students what they want most: Acceptance, Belonging, and Competence. It's about choosing to be engaged with the home, including parents, grandparents, and siblings.

One of the ways in which you can be purposeful is in your use of the handwritten note. It's a powerful tool in your teacher toolbelt, so use it often. These days, no one gets many handwritten notes in the mail. On those rare occasions that you do, you're likely impressed because such notes show extra effort. They're not emails or texts you can dash off in a few seconds. You have to find or buy a stamp. There's something about seeing writing on paper, too, to give it a weighty feel of permanence.

> Education isn't just a day job. It's about setting an atmosphere where students are actively engaged in their own learning, and parents are informed, supportive partners.

People in general pay far more attention to handwritten notes than to texts or emails. The effects of handwritten messages can be profound and lasting. Several years later one school is still talking about the student teacher who, on her last day, handed personalized handwritten notes with a smile and a thank you to every person who had assisted her on her journey at that school. The recipients included her supervising teacher, multiple other teachers who had observed her and given her ideas, staff members, administrators, the janitor, and two parent volunteers in her classroom.

To use this power of the note to its maximum, share specifics. General thank yous don't have the same meaningful and lasting effects. An example of specifics would be, "I see such a change in Gianna. This week she completed her homework and met every assignment deadline. Thank you for partnering with me in coming up with such a creative solution!" On a positive note, an exclamation mark or two can work in your favor. Above all, be encouraging. Take the time to say exactly what you want to say and reread the message before you seal that envelope.

> The effects of handwritten messages can be profound and lasting.

#2: Be persistent.

As the old saying goes, "Rome wasn't built in a day." Neither are relationships with parents of your students. Some parents are a breeze. Others simply aren't easy to deal with, no matter what you do. Ditto with some of your students in the beginning. But good things come to those who are both patient and tenacious in their pursuit.

If you want to get to know your parents, you need to go out of your way to make contact with them. Send an encouraging note, email, or text. Leave a brief phone message to say you're glad their son or daughter is in your class. Whet their curiosity a little. Then go to where they are after school in their cars, trucks, and SUVs. Accompany students out to the sidewalk as they arrive and leave. Your presence, friendly wave, and a few words will go a long way in cementing parents' beliefs that not only are you in their student's court, but you like the family too.

#3: Be positive.

Ever hear the folksy saying, "You can catch more flies with honey than with vinegar?" It's true. People flock around a person who is positive, while they run from a person who is negative.

One surefire way to get the year off on the right foot is to make a positive phone call. Sounds easy, doesn't it? And it's a great way to build relationships with your students' parents.

We highly recommend that you make calling each student's home within the first two weeks of school the *norm* in your schedule. Share one positive thing you have observed or experienced with their student. For example, "It's a pleasure to have Theodore in my class. He appears to be developing well in the area of science, which you were concerned about. I'm impressed with his efforts and also how polite he is. If something comes up that you want to talk about, I'm available." Sure, you handed out a sheet with your contact information and times available for after-school in-person conferences, but you can't count on every parent being as organized as you are.

If Gabriel is hyperactive in your class and keeps *you* energized merely coming up with creative ways to channel his energy into learning, you can still say: "I am looking forward to a great year with Gabriel. He brings a lot of energy to the classroom." That's the truth, and it's also positive.

Why is this so important? Many families only get that school phone call if there is an issue, a disciplinary action pending, or a negative comment to share. But a positive phone call is proactive. It helps families get to know you and your heart for students. It gives you a glimpse into your students' home life. It helps you establish the foundation of your relationship now, before any issues might crop up that you need to handle with the parent. As communication begins to flow, the partnership between school and home starts to blossom.

Depending on your teaching situation, you may not have the same level of support from the home. Don't let that deter you from making a positive phone call. Continue to offer your partnership even if it is turned down or there is little return from the parent side.

> ## *To Ponder...*
> Every day, every hour, the parents are either passively or actively forming those habits in their children upon which, more than upon anything else, future character and conduct depend.
>
> Charlotte Mason

Don't wait for the potential specter of disciplinary action. Major on communication, communication, communication. This strategic act will only take you about 90 seconds with each parent. But the relational dividends are exponential. Never underestimate the power of a positive phone call at the first of the year...or anytime.

Good gossip is rare indeed in school or anywhere else. But there's great value in it. Imagine the child who overhears a parent or guardian talking about the note you sent. He'll be circling the clouds for hours afterward.

#4: Be professional.

My college baseball coach once said to me, "Leman, if you can't play third base, at least look like you can. Tuck your shirt in." He was quite the encouraging mentor, but he did have a point. Do everything you can to appear as a professional. Dress professionally for Back-to-School Night and parent-teacher conferences. It might be tempting to wear a palate of colors if you are a kindergarten teacher deep into a flower-art paint project with your students, but simplify the wardrobe so you don't look like a circus. Then again, if you're a math teacher, a plain white shirt tucked into black pants might send the message, "I am boring. My subject is boring." Find a happy, professional medium.

Being professional doesn't only span your clothing choices. It has to do with the words you choose to use, how you greet people, the gestures you use, the tone of your emails and other communications, and so much more. When you are both professional and relational, parents will not only take you seriously but are more likely to think you'll get the job done well.

> When you are both professional and relational, parents will not only take you seriously but are more likely to think you'll get the job done well.

#5: Be proactive.

Have you ever found yourself in an email exchange that is accomplishing little or nothing except upping the ante on a concern? The replies continue to be fired back between the teacher and parent, but there is no resolution. Emotions on both sides rise. The issue negatively affecting the student, his performance, and his relationships at school is usually caught in the crossfire.

Engaging in an email battle on a specific issue related to a student leads teachers and parents nowhere fast. Why? Tone of voice is very hard to interpret through email. There are no visual cues such as body language and facial expressions to aid in discerning the level of concern. Email exchanges lack the give-and-take of a phone call or, better yet, an in-person conversation. Emails also lack the ability to clarify without sounding defensive or offensive. They cannot showcase reflective listening on both sides to better understand what the issue is.

Every teacher probably can recall receiving an angry email from a parent and trying to put out the fire without raising their own internal heat. Most of those issues could likely have been solved through a proactive phone call before they escalated. That was true for me when I received such an email but chose to phone instead of hitting "reply" on the email to the parent. My action of kindly greeting the parent with a calm voice and asking for clarification of the issue diffused the situation in minutes.

That exchange also taught me more than the power of the phone call. It encouraged me to pause and reconsider my homework assignments. Were they really the best choice for young second-graders if a mom was so frazzled that she felt led to pay an older sibling to do the assignment?

I reflected on alternate ways to encourage reading and eliminated the need to "do something" after reading a book. Maybe my students could read for the joy of reading without having to make a diorama, book report, oral presentation, or any other presentation afterward. Because I looked for growth and refinement in my own teaching practices, in the end I was thankful for the exchange I had with this family. As you partner with parents, be open to your own learning.

An Apple a Day

Send a friendly email once a month with classroom news and helpful tips. This assists in a steady flow of communication and ensures all parents have the same information. You can also explain concepts you are working on in the classroom, such as responsibility and accountability.

Some of the best overall advice we can give about becoming a great teacher by Friday can be stated in two words: be proactive. Be proactive in establishing your foundation, as we explored on Monday. Be proactive in managing your classroom and crafting its atmosphere, as we discussed on Tuesday. Be proactive in viewing your students as individuals and getting to know them in order to build a classroom community, as explored on Wednesday. Be proactive in letting the reality of consequences be the teacher and using relational discipline, as discussed on Thursday. Finally, be proactive in partnering with the home, as we are exploring in this Friday chapter. On top of that, never forget, in all that you do, lavish on the 3 Rs: Relationship, Relationship, Relationship.

If you are proactive and focus on relationships, you won't react to situations. You'll respond to them. You won't be on the defensive. You'll look for win-win solutions.

Top 10 Ways to Successfully Partner with Parents

1. Get to know them. Invite them into your class.

2. Be welcoming and accessible.

3. Send positive notes and call with positive experiences.

4. Return calls and emails within 24 hours.

5. Always start with a positive statement at any conference, phone chat, or face-to-face conversation.

6. Listen well and paraphrase back using "I" statements. "I hear you saying that…"

7. Involve them in problem-solving.

8. Communicate, communicate, communicate.

9. When in doubt, don't email. Pick up the phone and call.

10. Go the extra mile. Be all about customer service.

If you major on the 3 Rs and focus on the 5 Ps, you can get off on the right foot every year and smooth that pathway for the rest of the year. So, send that welcome letter several weeks before school starts. Use Back-to-School Night (or craft a similar get-together if your school does not have one) to inform, encourage, and lay the bricks for a healthy partnership between school and home. Engage with parents. Listen, listen, and listen some more. Follow up within 24 hours with any parents who have mentioned challenges at home and want to discuss concerns. The more equipped you are when that child walks through the door the first day of school, the better.

Using the 5 Ps in your teacher-home partnership from that first day of school forward will prompt a natural flow of communication. When you use them consistently, the time you invest is much smaller than you might think, but it'll reap so many benefits. You'll have a smooth-running classroom without parental interruptions. Parents will be well-informed about what's going on in the classroom and confident that you have their child's best in mind. You will learn more about your students' lives at home in order to motivate them and solve issues as they arise. Most of all, you'll have established a solid foundation for your parent-teacher-student relationship trio that can weather any storm that might arise during the school year.

An Apple a Day

What Would You Do If...?

For each scenario, think of a "5 Ps" solution: **P**urposeful, **P**ersistent, **P**ositive, **P**rofessional, and **P**roactive. For additional perspective and ideas, brainstorm with another teacher.

Scenario #1: A parent seems to be avoiding you. He missed the parent-teacher conference. You have concerns that you would like to address but are having a hard time getting the parent to come in. What do you do?

Scenario #2: A student in your class has been struggling socially. You have tried to encourage this student to make better choices. The parents are concerned about all the notes and emails regarding their child's behavior.

At recess you notice the student making positive choices that reflect your expectations. What do you do?

Scenario #3: Your student's mother has scheduled a meeting for this afternoon, but she has given you no indication of what she wants to talk about. Her child is doing very well academically and socially, so you don't have a clue as to the topic. At the appointed time, Mom enters your classroom, sits down, and begins to tell you that she feels you need to present your class lessons in a different way and that your curriculum could be improved. What do you do?

Scenario #4: It happens every morning like clockwork. The students have already lined up, and Ms. Talker is at your line once again. She is pleasant but insistent as she catches your eye and smilingly demands your attention: "This will only take a second." Of course, it never does. The topic doesn't really matter, either. She only wants to chat. Always the professional, you give her your attention. By the third day, however, you begin to resent the daily intrusion and realize you have a problem on your hands. What do you do?

Scenario #5: Mr. Tate comes into your classroom without warning, visibly upset. "You are giving out too much homework," he fumes. "Really, it is ridiculous what he has to do. I don't have time for it. I work all day and come home late. By the time I feed him, he has only half an hour to do his homework before bedtime. He has enough school all day. Why does he have to do more? Are you not doing your job? Is that why you have to give out so much homework? What is the reason? I'd like an answer!" What do you do?

Scenario #6: The day after report cards go home, Ms. Smith calls you, clearly upset. "My child received straight As on her last report card," she says. "Now it's mostly Bs and Cs. What is going on? Why didn't you let me know? We need to meet immediately to discuss this." What do you do?

Scenario #7: You repeatedly ask a student to put the basketball away and stop playing with it in the halls and your classroom. The student responds to your request with, "If you take my basketball, I will call the police." You end up taking the basketball and sending it to the office so the parent can pick it up. Mom arrives and is upset because she "has no time to deal with this." What do you do?

Scenario #8: A student has been struggling academically. Through hard work and determination, you see the grades are steadily improving. What do you do?

Your Mighty Role as Advocate and Ambassador

What kids see, they will model. Parents—including those who are overly busy or absent—are 24/7 teachers of values and priorities. That's why every interaction you have with students and their parents is a potential ground-breaker. You influence more than students when you partner with the home; you also influence parents and the way in which they parent.

Consider the top complaints middle-schoolers have about parents:

- They don't understand me or the world I live in.

- They never listen.

- All they care about is if I do my chores on time and keep my room clean.

- Dad's never around.

- Mom's too busy to talk.

When you ask parents questions about their child and seek to understand their home life and world so you can better assist that child, you model how parents could tackle the first complaint. When you listen to and communicate with parents, you model how to address the second complaint. When you act as a child's advocate and dig in to find out what interests her and care about her heart, you model how to care about the whole child, not merely her actions. When you consistently show up at the sidewalk and to your students' after-school activities to cheer them on, you plant a seed for how life could be different at that house if Dad's priorities shifted. And finally, your words to that parent, "If you ever have any concerns or questions, contact me. I'd be happy to talk," model consistent relational caring that could revamp the home life of that student if Mom took it to heart.

You also choose to model values and priorities in so many other ways.

#1: You choose to be approachable.

You honestly state that you don't know everything. You are a life-long learner. You're a great listener and have an inquiring mind. You are transparent: you say what you mean and mean what you say. You have a sense of humor when situations go awry and can laugh at yourself. You are humble, teachable, and can admit when you make a mistake or interpret a situation incorrectly because you did not take time to gather all the information.

#2: You choose to respond, instead of react.

You know that reacting is easy in the moment. You don't have to think. You simply let the words or actions fly. The problem is, the fallout is weighty. You are emotionally distressed and now have the grand opportunity to apologize. As an authoritative teacher who focuses on the 3 Rs and the 5 Ps, you're now learning to take the higher ground. That means thinking through what you will say, how you will say it, the consequences of what you will say, and then adjusting your words and actions accordingly.

#3: You choose to love unconditionally.

That means loving students and parents who aren't easy to love and who may have a reputation for being difficult. But you do so because you have the long-term picture and potential benefits in mind. They're worth any effort you can give.

Take Asher and his father, for instance. Everyone in their small town considered Asher a juvenile delinquent with a dead-beat dad and no mom anywhere on the horizon. But his teacher refused to hear those words. She was determined to find the good in that 13-year-old student everyone rolled their eyes about. When she discovered that his classmates were teasing him about being dumb and unable to read, she pulled him aside privately. With a friendly smile she offered to supply a snack after school. You see, this teacher was observant and had noticed his lunches seemed slim for a growing boy.

That day Asher exited the classroom with the other students as usual, loitered in the hallway for about 10 minutes, and then came in to sit down. Teacher and student ate together. She asked him about his hobbies and interests.

He lit up. "Motorcycles."

They had a lengthy conversation about why he loved motorcycles and what he knew about them. Then she said calmly, "I know your classmates are teasing you about struggling with reading. That must be hard. If you ever want to share anything with me, I'm here, and I'd be happy to hear it. I'd also like to help if I can."

She didn't expect a response since Asher was mostly silent in class. But he surprised her with his comment and the velocity of it: "I'm not dumb!"

He'd opened up his feelings on the subject all on his own. By the end of their conversation, the snacks were gone, and they had a plan, as long as Asher's father agreed. The teacher phoned Asher's father that night. His tone was gruff and dismissive at first, but she powered on with her request.

To her surprise, the dad quickly agreed, but with a condition: "I can't pay you, but I can bring you fresh produce from our garden." She enthusiastically accepted the condition. Being paid was never her interest, but she knew she had to win the father's cooperation. With his permission, she tutored Asher privately half an hour after school each day for three months.

Asher tested her grace and her patience numerous times. Once he threw a rock at a window in her house and yelled that she was a mean teacher. But she persisted. What had looked like squiggles to a reluctant reader now started to take shape as words.

Their relational circle of trust as student, teacher, and parent slowly developed. Asher's dad now confidently stopped by her house every week or two to give her a tray of vegetables he had arranged artistically. She found out that he was a jack-of-all trades who had never finished eighth grade because of family circumstances.

At the three-month mark, the usually late-to-school Asher burst through her classroom door 15 minutes early. "Mrs. C, I can read!" he exclaimed. "This says…" He rushed over to her, jabbed his finger at a page, and slowly read the entire page of a nonfiction book about motorcycle repair that he'd checked out of the local library. That was the turning point for Asher and for his dad, who was also embarrassed by the fact that he couldn't read.

> Their relational circle of trust as student, teacher, and parent slowly developed.

Six years later, guess what Asher was doing? He was repairing local motorcycles with his dad to earn money to go part-time to a technical college to learn more about that trade. Further, guess who was reading the repair manuals? *Both* of them.

As teachers partner with parents, they not only become advocates for the students in their class. They also become ambassadors with family-changing potential. Asher and his dad are living proof.

Powerful transformation can occur when a teacher is **P**urposeful, **P**ersistent, **P**ositive, **P**rofessional, and **P**roactive. Pair those 5 Ps with the 3 Rs, and you've got a winning combination for success at school and for a lifetime. We can't wait to see how they will spark world-changing potential.

Decide Your Legacy

All of us will leave an imprint.
What will yours be?

When I was in fifth grade, I hated reading because I struggled with English Language Arts (ELA) skills. I remember viewing the word *island* and pronouncing it "is-land." The minute the word came out of my mouth, I knew it did not sound right. How did the other kids know the word was *island?* All I saw was "is-land," never understanding the "s" was silent. Was I just dumb?

Then Ms. Jeannie Tompkins, a soft-spoken, patient, and very kind tutor entered my life. She cared for me as a person *first,* then worked on my lacking ELA skills. Despite my academic shortcomings, she accepted me for who I was and made it a priority to make me feel special and accepted. Because of my relationship with Ms. Tompkins, I worked hard. I learned how to say *island* properly.

I also learned the value of that hard work and perseverance, skills I treasure to this day. Regardless of the obstacles ahead, I have become a person who doesn't give up or give in. Instead I find a way to solve the problem, like Ms. Tompkins did. Also because of her, I have great empathy for students who struggle in their younger years with *any* academic subject. I compassionately support them as people first and then look for strategies to empower them to be successful in achieving their personal bests. In short, that tutor provided me a lifetime legacy that I am able to pass on to my own students.

Every single person on planet Earth will leave an imprint of some kind. It's impossible to be neutral. What kind of teacher do you want to be? What legacy do you want to leave behind?

Will you be the teacher a student talks about years later? The one who motivated her? Who treated him as something other than a troublemaker when everyone else called him "impossible"? Who listened and encouraged her during a tough time? Who pointed out a surprise skill that directed his path in life? Who was known for being the trusted teacher whom colleagues could go to for advice, empathy, and not judgment? Who assisted administration in turning around a toxic school environment into a beneficial-for-all one?

To become a great teacher by Friday, you need three things: a passion for education, a healthy dose of selflessness, and a personal growth mindset.

Remember the ABCs

Teaching isn't just a career you might have for a lifetime. It's about changing others' lifetimes. Both of us are living proof of teachers who believed in us, encouraged us, and supported us in our journeys.

> Teaching isn't just a career you might have for a lifetime. It's about changing others' lifetimes.

All children want to be accepted by those who matter to them. They want to belong to a community. And they want to be seen as competent and able to give back to that community.

There are students who are loved at home who come to school to learn. There

162

are also students who are not loved at home who come to school to be loved. They must be loved before they can learn.

The next time a child rushes in to your class, waves her homework in your direction, and calls out, "Look what I did!" she needs your attention. Not only is she showing interest and ownership in her project, she's clearly longing for a recognition of her efforts that she may not get at home. Will you be the teacher who stops for a minute and says with a smile, "Oh, let me take a look at that! ... Well, your hard work is certainly paying off. You were able to answer all the math problems this time. That must feel really good."

It only takes a minute or two to invest in a child's world, and the dividends are out of this world.

> There are students who are loved at home who come to school to learn. There are also students who are not loved at home who come to school to be loved. They must be loved before they can learn.

The JOY Club

When I was young, my mother signed me up for something called JOY Club. I hated every minute of it. It was held in the basement of a woman's home with the sole entertainment being some really old-fashioned flannel graph figures. If they were teaching the ancient story about baby Moses discovered in a basket in the bulrushes, you'd be lucky to have a few cattails on the flannel graph.

Somehow such visuals were supposed to capture and keep the attention of very active young boys like myself. I'll tell you, that JOY Club was the most boring club ever. However, to this day, I remember what the JOY stood for: *Jesus, Others, You.*

What does this have to do with teaching? Well, notice that the *You* is last. In teaching, you have to focus on the student first, the student's family second, and then yourself as the conduit of learning. In some situations, that's very hard. No doubt, you've already faced some of those tough times if you've been in the field for at least a year.

But the benefits to this relational approach are many. You won't spend your time being frustrated or offended when events occur, as they always will. Instead of allowing your blood pressure to rise due to a recalcitrant student, your relational wisdom will kick in. You'll pull that student aside and calmly work to identify the purpose of that behavior.

When you receive a snippy phone call, text, or email from a parent, you won't take it personally. Instead, you'll calmly contact the parent and begin problem-solving to get to the root of the matter. As we've discovered, missiles directed at teachers often have little or nothing to do with the teacher or their teaching. They have everything to do with a parent's stress, fear, guilt, and anger over situations happening outside of school.

Only if you get this order right will teaching transform from just a job to a joy. Then you'll have the opportunity to become the difference-maker you crave to be.

A Growth Mindset

What is a growth mindset, and how can you develop it? When you have a growth mindset, you're eager to learn from others. You are intensely curious. You ask questions, probe, and research. You welcome questions and suggestions. You visit other classrooms, observe masterful teachers, and reflect on what you've learned. You enjoy employing new methods in the classroom and are comfortable in sharing your struggles and successes in an effort to grow.

You avidly seek out other teachers who have different strengths than your own. You might ask how a colleague managed to teach a difficult concept. You pursue new ideas so you can excel at the art of teaching because you know the high stakes.

> ### *To Ponder...*
>
> Life as a teacher begins the day
> that you realize that you are always a learner.
>
> ROBERT JOHN MEEHAN

You share resources willingly and allow other teachers to learn from you. You don't need ownership over your ideas. You don't care about getting credit. Hearing that one of your ideas worked for another teacher is all the encouragement you need to power on.

You check in with colleagues from time to time. You welcome the new teacher down the hall and offer to be a sounding board any time. You spot another class engaged in an intriguing project and stop in later to inquire with the teacher how it went.

In everything you do, you focus on the 3 Rs. You greet other teachers in the hall and offer a happy word to start their day. You treat the janitor the same way you treat the principal, with respect and kindness. You park somewhere different two days a week so you can walk in and chat with different staff members. You acknowledge grandparents and parents in the hallways and welcome their contributions to your classroom. You use the power of a handwritten note to encourage others in the school community.

You model a positive attitude. Your heart bursts with gratitude for the chance to be a difference-maker in the lives of your students and their families. You feel truly called to be where you are right now, despite any current challenges.

What you've learned about yourself as a teacher in this book will establish a foundation for you to build a unique classroom tailored with your characteristic flair. It will also help to direct your efforts on your continuing educational journey. As a quote I used to hang on my desk by Joseph Joubert said, "To teach is to learn twice over."

Identifying areas in which you might be weak isn't an easy task, and we applaud your efforts. But here's the perk: once you know those weaknesses, you can work on ways to turn them into positive benefits for you and for your students. That's incredibly exciting.

But remember, cathedrals of excellence aren't built in a day...or even in five days. They are built brick by brick. Along the way, you'll likely have a few "whoops" with the hammer, have to adjust a board that's slightly out of plumb, and fill in a chink out of the mortar here or there. That's okay, and it's all a part of the building process.

You see, the best teachers aren't those who are perfect. They are the ones who have a growth mindset that energizes them for the long haul of teaching and drives them to do their personal best. They view themselves as lifelong learners, are reflective on their teaching practices, see opportunities for growth, and take advantage of them.

An Apple a Day

Maximize Your Impact

1. Identify areas where your contributions already shine brightly in your school community. Jot those down with a big smiley face next to them. Post that list where you will see it each day as encouragement.

2. Identify areas that could use your positive imprint. Jot those down under a "What if...?" heading. Brainstorm one way you could exert beneficial influence over one of those areas and try it out consistently over the next month.

3. At the end of the month evaluate yourself. If the "What if...?" area needs more work, try it for a

second month until it becomes natural. If you're satisfied you're positively contributing in that area, jot it down on your smiley-face page.

4. Repeat the exercise with other areas in which you could make a positive imprint.

The Final Word

Our own stories, and the transformation we've watched in the lives of countless other students, reveal the unparalleled opportunity that teachers have to impact the world. It starts with influencing a single child's world. Neither of us would be who we are today without the impact of those teachers who chose to be observant, patient, and kind, who worked to have a relationship with us, and who believed the best in us despite any evidence to the contrary.

You've done a lot of hard work in the last five days. Just look at what you've accomplished. It must feel really good. You've mastered education basics and figured out what school environment is a match for you. You've honed classroom management skills so you'll come off like a confident pro, plus created the kind of classroom culture where students actively want to engage in their own learning.

You've learned how to identify who your students are, what they need most, and how to uniquely motivate them. You've learned about relational discipline as the best game in town because it serves the ball of responsibility, accountability, and consequences solidly into a student's court while growing your relationship with that student. And, finally, you've discovered how the 5 Ps of home partnership prep the stage for a good year with students and their parents or guardians and also assist with any set changes that might need to occur during that year.

With those five winning plays, your passionate heart for educating children, and a growth mindset, your ability to change the world will be astounding. Fast forward 10-20 years, and you know who your students will be talking about as the change-maker in their lives?

You.

Top 15 Teacher Countdown

15. Make learning fun!

14. Pursue excellence, but never self-defeating perfection.

13. Be proactive and responsive, not reactive.

12. Remember that all behavior is purposeful.

11. Let reality do the talking (and disciplining).

10. Encourage, but never praise.

09. Win your students' cooperation.

08. Never do for a student what she can do for herself.

07. Remember what kids want most: the ABCs (Acceptance, Belonging, Competence).

06. Teach in such a way that every student believes he or she is your favorite.

05. Motivate students by knowing and understanding them as individuals.

04. Major on respect, responsibility, and accountability as classroom foundations.

03. Never pass your authority in the classroom to anyone else.

02. Use the power of positive expectations and slather on the vitamins and virtues.

01. Fine-tune your get-it skills, and the rest of your job will come much more easily.

Notes

1   Dorothy L. Sayers, "The Lost Tools of Learning," Speech (Oxford, UK: Oxford University, 1947), https://classicalchristian.org/the-lost-tools-of-learning-dorothy-sayers/.

2   "Praise," *Merriam-Webster Dictionary,* https://www.merriam-webster.com/dictionary/praise.

3   "Encouragement," *Oxford Languages,* https:///www.google.com/search?q=encouragement+definition.

4   "Encourage," *Merriam-Webster Dictionary,* https://www.merriam-webster.com/dictionary/encourage.

5   Haim G. Ginott, *Teacher and Child: A Book for Parents and Teachers* (New York: The Macmillan Company, 1972), preface, 15. See also "I Have Come to a Frightening Conclusion. I Am the Decisive Element in the Classroom," *Quote Investigator,* October 8, 2018, https://quoteinvestigator.com/2018/10/08/decisive/.

6   "Charlotte Mason Quotes and Sayings," *Inspiring Quotes,* https://www.inspiringquotes.us/author/8747-charlotte-mason.

7   "Madeline Hunter's Lesson Plan," Iowa State University, https://www2.econ.iastate.edu/classes/tsc220/hallam/MadelineHunterModel.pdf.

8   Robert J. Stahl, "Using 'Think-Time' and 'Wait-Time' Skillfully in the Classroom," *ERIC Digest,* (Bloomington, IN: ERIC Clearinghouse for Social Studies/Social Science, 1994-05-00), http://ocw.umb.edu/early-education-development/echd-440-640-eec-language-and-literacy-course/learning-module-1/module-5/Wait%20Time.pdf.

9   Ibid.

10   See Proverbs 14:29 in *The Holy Bible.*

11   Kyle Benson, "The Magic Relationship Ratio, According to Science," https://www.gottman.com/blog/the-magic-relationship-ratio-according-science/.

12   The four stages of misbehavior originated with the teaching of Alfred Adler, the father of Individual Psychology. They were further developed by Rudolph Dreikurs.

13   For more about the goals and stages of misbehavior, see Dr. Kevin Leman, *Parenting the Powerful Child* (Grand Rapids, MI: Revell, 2014).

14   Caitlin Dempsey, "The Largest Cactus in the United States," *Geographyrealm,* https://www.geographyrealm.com/the-largest-cactus-in-the-united-states/#.

15   For more on turning behavior around, see Dr. Kevin Leman, *Why Kids Misbehave: And What You Can Do About It* (Grand Rapids, MI: Revell, 2020).

Acknowledgments

To Mom and Dad:
You are my cherished teachers. I continue to learn from you.
Your unconditional support and belief in me
shaped me into the person I am today.
I love you and our special family.
—*Kristin Leman O'Reilly*

To our colleagues at Leman Academy of Excellence: Your dedication to your scholars and teaching is impressive. Thank you for your part in creating tomorrow's leaders today. It is our joy to work alongside you.

To teachers nationwide who give of themselves unconditionally for the betterment of others: Remember that all future occupations begin with a teacher. You are doing a life-changing work.

To Ramona Tucker: Thanks for fiercely fighting for this book to be published and walking alongside us in the process.

About
Dr. Kevin Leman

An internationally known psychologist, radio and television personality, educator, speaker, and humorist, Dr. Kevin Leman has taught and entertained audiences worldwide with his wit and commonsense psychology.

The *New York Times* bestselling and award-winning author of over 70 titles on parenting, marriage, family, and education, including *The Birth Order Book, Have a New Kid by Friday, Sheet Music, Making Children Mind without Losing Yours, Parenting the Powerful Child, Be the Dad She Needs You to Be, The Way of the Shepherd, 8 Secrets to Raising Successful Kids, 7 Things He'll Never Tell You but You Need to Know, Education a la Carte, Why Kids Misbehave,* and *Planet Middle School,* Dr. Leman has made thousands of house calls through radio and television programs, including *FOX & Friends,* Hallmark Channel's *Home & Family, The View,* FOX's *The Morning Show, Today,* Dr. Bill Bennett's *Morning in America, The List, Today, Oprah, The 700 Club,* CBS's *The Early Show,* CNN, and *Focus on the Family.*

Dr. Leman has served as a contributing family psychologist to *Good Morning America.* He frequently speaks to schools, CEO groups, businesses—including Fortune 500 companies and others such as YPO, Million Dollar Round Table, and Top of the Table—and civic and church organizations. A practicing psychologist for over 40 years, Dr. Kevin Leman has helped millions of adults understand the dynamics of healthy relationships.

His professional affiliations include the American Psychological Association and the North American Society of Adlerian Psychology. He received the Distinguished Alumnus Award (1993) and an honorary Doctor of Humane Letters degree (2010) from North Park University, and a bachelor's degree in psychology, his master's and doctorate degrees, as well as the Alumni Achievement Award (2003)—the highest award they can give one of their own—from the University of Arizona. Dr. Leman is the founder of Leman Academy of Excellence (www.lemanacademy.com).

Originally from Williamsville, New York, Dr. Leman and his wife, Sande, live in Tucson, Arizona, and have five children and four grandchildren.

If you're looking for an entertaining speaker for your event or fund-raiser, please contact:

Dr. Kevin Leman
PO Box 35370
Tucson, Arizona 85740
Phone: (520) 797-3830
www.birthorderguy.com

Follow Dr. Kevin Leman on Facebook (facebook.com/DrKevinLeman) and on X (@DrKevinLeman). Check out the free podcasts at birthorderguy.com/podcast.

For "Dr. Kevin Leman" resources on marriage, parenting, family, education, and many other topics: go to amazon.com.

For more about Leman Academy of Excellence visit lemanacademy.com.

About
Kristin Leman O'Reilly

As the Director of Curriculum and Instruction at the award-winning Leman Academy of Excellence—a public, classical, charter school with nine campuses throughout Arizona and Colorado—Kristin Leman O'Reilly oversees curriculum and the Leman educational philosophy.

Kristin began her educational journey nearly three decades ago and has an M.A. in Teaching, B.A. in Elementary Education, and a B.A. in Psychology. She has taught in both private and charter schools, holding various leadership roles as Curriculum Coordinator, Professional Development Administrator, and Vice Principal.

She is passionate about mentoring teachers and training them to be lifelong learners to inspire the next generation of leaders. She created the Teacher Recognition Program at Leman Academy to honor teachers and shower them with the appreciation they deserve. She annually trains nearly 400 incoming and resident Leman Academy teachers, as well as supporting them throughout the year with ongoing Professional Development workshops.

Kristin, her husband, Dennis, and children, Conner and Adeline, reside in Tucson, Arizona.